STUDIES IN CHURCH HISTORY

THE CHRISTIAN CHURCH IN THE EPISTLES OF ST. JEROME

BY THE REV.
L. HUGHES, M.A., D.D.
VICAR OF SAFFRON WALDEN

WIPF & STOCK · Eugene, Oregon

Wipf and Stock Publishers
199 W 8th Ave, Suite 3
Eugene, OR 97401

The Christian Church in the Epistle of St. Jerome
By Hughes, Leonard
ISBN 13: 978-1-62032-383-0
Publication date 6/21/2012
Previously published by SPCK, 1923

CONTENTS

		PAGE
INTRODUCTION		vii

I. THE CLERGY:
- (a) Morals ... 1
- (b) Grades and Ranks ... 10
- (c) Diaconate's Importance ... 11
- (d) Relation of Episcopate to Presbyterate ... 11
- (e) Case of Alexandria ... 13

II. THE SCRIPTURES:
- (a) Wide study of ... 20
- (b) State of the Text ... 24
- (c) Jerome's Version; its Difficulties and Principles; Merits of the Vulgate ... 25

III. THE ASCETIC AND MONASTIC MOVEMENT ... 38

IV. ROME AND THE ROMAN SEE ... 55

V. THE PROGRESS OF THE CHURCH ... 64

VI. HERESIES AND SCHISMS ... 73
- (a) Montanism ... 74
- (b) Origenism ... 79
- (c) Pelagianism ... 88

VII. DOCTRINE AND PRACTICE ... 98
- (a) Eucharist ... 98
- (b) Baptism ... 101
- (c) Relics ... 103
- (d) Pilgrimages ... 104
- (e) Miscellaneous ... 105

VIII. CONCLUSION ... 107

THE FOLLOWING BOOKS HAVE BEEN CONSULTED IN THE PREPARATION OF THIS WORK

1. J. P. MIGNE, "Patrologiae Cursus Completus Latinae." Vol. XXII.
2. "Cambridge Mediaeval History." Vol. I.
3. S. DILL, "Roman Society in the Last Century of the Western Empire." Second edition.
4. W. H. FREMANTLE, "Letters of St. Jerome." Wace and Schaff's Nicene and Post-Nicene Library.
5. E. GIBBON, "Decline and Fall of the Roman Empire." Vols. III. and IV.
6. T. R. GLOVER, "Life and Letters in the Fourth Century."
7. C. GORE, "The Church and the Ministry." Second edition.
8. F. GREGOROVIUS, "Rome in the Middle Ages." Vol. I., translated by G. Hamilton.
9. J. HASTINGS, "Dictionary of the Bible." Vol. IV., Article "Vulgate" (H. J. White).
10. B. J. KIDD, "A History of the Church." Vols. I., II., and III.
11. MARCELLINUS (AMMIANUS), "Quae Supersunt." Editio Tauchnitziana, Lipsiae.
12. H. H. MILMAN, "History of Latin Christianity." Vol. I.
13. H. H. MILMAN, "History of Christianity." Vol. III.
14. W. SMITH, "Dictionary of the Bible." Vol. III., Article "Vulgate" (Westcott).
15. J. WORDSWORTH, "Ministry of Grace."
16. WORDSWORTH AND WHITE, "Novum Testamentum Domini Nostri Jesu Christi Latine," Secundum Editionem S. Hieronymi.

INTRODUCTION

THE letters of a man who has held high office in Church or State, while not a deliberate, systematic chronicle of events, may yet be worthy of study by reason of the side-lights they throw on the history of the time. The correspondence, *e.g.*, of Pliny, Ignatius, Oliver Cromwell, Horace Walpole, and of many others, is all of admitted value for such a purpose. Nor is it otherwise with the epistles of St. Jerome. One of the outstanding figures of the fourth and fifth centuries A.D., he struck in a special degree the imagination of his contemporaries. He had, indeed, many claims to their attention. He was well acquainted with classical literature, and his works abound in quotations from Virgil, Plato, Persius, Plautus, Quintilian, Cicero. He had a vivid and vigorous style, and the pen of a ready writer, a pen dipped sometimes very deeply in the gall of bitterness. Like the prophet Isaiah, he was a keen observer of feminine vanities and extravagance. Above all, he was in close touch in his cell at Bethlehem with both East and West, and those who sought his counsel were mainly men and women of noble birth or of good education. The letters of such a man are necessarily of much interest to the student, and the correspondence of so compelling a personality can scarcely fail to be of service in ascertaining the actual conditions of Church life in his day.

THE CHRISTIAN CHURCH IN THE EPISTLES OF ST. JEROME

I

THE CLERGY

(a) MORALS

ST. JEROME'S description of the clergy of his time is, in many respects, far from flattering, and if it be true to any serious extent, it implies a marked falling off in their general character. Letter xxii. 28, *e.g.*, is a grave indictment of the Christian Ministry in the closing years of the fourth century.

"There are others—I speak of those of my own order—who seek the presbyterate and the diaconate in order to see women with less restraint. Such men are entirely engrossed with their dress; whether their perfumes are sufficiently fragrant and whether there are any creases in their shoes. Their hair bears evident traces of curling-tongs; their fingers glisten with rings; they walk lightly on tip-toe lest wet roads should splash their feet. Such men, when you see them, you would fancy to be bridegrooms rather than clergy. Some of them have devoted all their energies, nay their very life, to the one single

2   THE EPISTLES OF ST. JEROME

object of knowing the names, houses, and characters of married ladies. One of these clerics, the head of the profession, I will briefly and summarily describe, that from the master you may the more easily recognise the disciples. He gets up hurriedly at sunrise, arranges the order of his visits, takes the shortest roads, and—tiresome old man that he is—forces his way almost to the very bedchambers of ladies still asleep. Should he see a little cushion that takes his fancy, or a smart table-cover, or any other article of household furniture, he praises it, looks at it with admiration, handles it, and, complaining that he himself has nothing like it, extorts rather than begs it from the owner, for every lady fears to give offence to the newsmonger * of the town. To him chastity and fasting are equally repugnant, whereas a savoury breakfast is much to his liking—so also is a fat young crane,† of the kind commonly called a chirper.‡ In speech he is uncouth and forward and is always ready for wrangling. Wherever you turn, he is the first man you meet. Whatever news is bruited abroad, he is either the inventor or exaggerator of the report. His horses are changed every hour and are so sleek and spirited that you would deem him a brother of (Diomede) the Thracian King."

Side by side with the foregoing may be set various sections of letter lii. From lii. 5, it seems that there were clerics engaged in business who had risen thereby from poverty to wealth and from obscurity to prominence whom Nepotian is told to avoid like the plague.

---

* *Veredarius* = a postboy or courier—" used comically of a priest eager for gossip " (Lewis and Short) ; said to be derived from Veho and Rheda (a four-wheeled carriage).

† *Geranopepa* = a very difficult and possibly corrupt term. Erasmus conjectures either γερανοπέπτα, *i.e.* cooked crane, or γερανοκόπτα, *i.e.* crane cut up in small pieces.

‡ *Pipizo* = from pipio, to peep or chirp.

THE CLERGY

Paragraph 16 of the same epistle declares that other priests were stewards and managers of estates and households. Paragraph 6 speaks of clergy born in country cottages, who once knew what it was to be short even of the peasant's humble black bread, but who had become epicures of the superlative degree, fastidious as to the finest wheat-flour and honey, quick to tell by the flavour from what coast or province their fish or game had come. Others show a fawning servility to childless old men and women for whom in their sickness they perform the most menial and revolting offices. Indeed, so greedy were the pastors of the Church that Valentinian I. in 370, in an edict addressed to Pope Damasus, prohibited ecclesiastics from entering the houses of wards and widows, and made illegal both " donatio inter vivos " and testamentary bequests to the Church. This law, however, was largely defeated by the device of a fictitious trusteeship (" per fidei commissa legibus illudimus "). Jerome makes no complaint of the actual provisions of the edict, but laments the fact that such legislation should be necessary (" nec de lege conqueror, sed doleo cur meruerimus hanc legem ").

Similarly in cxxx. 7, he asserts that while devout women like Proba were *selling* estates, ecclesiastics were *buying* them.

But, according to Jerome, the clergy were infected not only with worldliness and avarice, but with vanity also. Their preaching was not always aimed at the conversion and edification of their hearers, but sometimes at any rate to win applause from the congregation. Even, it seems, the great Gregory of Nazianzus was not superior to " ad captandum " tricks of oratory. In lii. 8, Jerome relates how he once asked him to explain the meaning of " sabbatum δευτερόπρωτον," and how Gregory replied that he would do so in church and that the people—Jerome included—would applaud his interpretation.

Again, Vigilantius had once applauded a sermon by Jerome on the Resurrection—in fact, all the great preachers of the time, Paul of Samosata, Chrysostom, Theodoret, etc., were constantly so treated—a custom which Augustine once, at any rate, utilised for rebuke: "You have applauded. It pains me. Your plaudits are leaves. I want fruit" (Sermo lxi. 13).

Indeed, so common had the practice become that Jerome in his preface to his commentary on the Galatians, says: "We meet as if we were in the Athenaeum or lecture-room to kindle the applause of the bystanders."

Looking back over these statements as to the personal character of the clergy of the time, one feels that the picture is not pleasing, and the question at once arises as to what foundation there is for it in fact, and whether or not it is corroborated by outside testimony. As far back as 325 the seventeenth Canon of the Council of Nicaea reproved the rapacity of the clergy and denounced clerical usurers. The law of Valentinian half a century later is an ugly fact, the meaning of which is unmistakable. A little later still Chrysostom finds that the clergy of Constantinople, under the lax administration of Nectarius, had gravely deteriorated, and is compelled to depose two deacons for serious offences and to repel other clergy from the Eucharist. Six eastern bishops are

THE CLERGY

deposed for simony—indeed the avarice, indolence, and immorality of the ministry tried Chrysostom to the uttermost. Jerome then, as far as the Eastern Church is concerned, is not without support for his statements on the subject. The " veredarius urbis " of whom he writes so caustically in letter xxii. is clearly drawn from life. No writer, even though endowed with the vivid imagination of Jerome, could entirely invent such a personage. He claims, indeed, to paint the portrait " quo facilius magistro cognito discipulos recognoscas," but it is hard to believe that such " discipuli " were at all numerous or sunk so deep in foppery and greed as the " magister." It seems impossible that the clergy had so greatly and so generally deteriorated in the course of half a century. Fifty years before, Constantine had given them an " exemptio " to trade untaxed because their profits might be given to the poor, while it is notorious that they were always ready to convert communion plate into money for the relief of distress and the ransom of prisoners. Julian the Apostate, too, paid the ministry of the Church a very high tribute when he required his pagan priests to imitate their gravity and purity of life and still more their charity and benevolence to the poor. Augustine when Bishop of Hippo not only had a careful audit of the Church accounts, but also would never accept a bequest if to do so meant suffering to the testator's family. While, therefore, Jerome's " Veredarius " is doubtless an historical person, he can hardly be accepted as a type of the Christian ministry as a whole. Much of what Jerome says as to clerical greed is based only on hearsay evidence. His account of the legacy-hunting priests in lii. 6, discharging the most disgusting duties of an attendant on the sick is, after all, only a report ("*Audio* praeterea in senes et anus absque liberis," etc.), and rumour is ever unkind. The assertion, too, in cxxx. 7, that Proba was selling property while the clergy were buying, rests only on a "dicitur," and the words in the same passage, "omnis ecclesiastici ministerii gradus," have about them a decided ring of exaggeration.

Mr. Stewart, in the "Cambridge Mediaeval History," vol. i. p. 591, remarks with truth that, Valentinian's edict notwithstanding, the Church's "growing wealth was, as a rule, generously applied to philanthropic work started by the Church, and Augustine was justified in calling upon Churchmen to remember Christ as well as their sons."

Apparently, insufficient care was exercised by the bishops in the choice of ordinands.

In lii. 10 Jerome complains that while altars were studded with jewels, no regard was paid to the choice of ministers; and again, Adv. Jovinian i. 34,

"bishops choose into the ranks of the clergy not the best but the cleverest men . . . or as though they were distributing the offices of an earthly service, they give posts to their kindred and relations, or they listen to the dictates of wealth, and, worse than all, they give promotion to those who besmear them with flattery."

Though there is a rhetorical ring about these passages, they seem to be confirmed to some extent by Jerome's contemporary, Chrysostom. In his treatise "de Sacerdotio," which Dr. J. A. Nairn believes to have

THE CLERGY

been written in 387, he insists on the solemn responsibility of those who confer ordination. It is no excuse to say they were unacquainted with him they admitted to the ministry, but rather a ground of condemnation. Men buying a slave take all manner of precautions ; they show him to doctors, require sureties, make full inquiry of neighbours, and take him for a time on trial before completing the purchase. Still more is it necessary to take every care in ordination ; candidates must not be accepted lightly or heedlessly, or on a certificate given through partiality and received without further inquiry.

Such warnings are not likely to have been given without cause. Painful experience had almost certainly shown their necessity. St. Paul's rule to Timothy had evidently not been acted upon with sufficient strictness at the close of the fourth century —χεῖρας ταχέως μηδενὶ ἐπιτίθει.

Such carelessness may in part at any rate account not only for the alleged avarice and worldliness, but for the far worse vices which Jerome attributes to the clergy of his day. There is, *e.g.*, the gross scandal —the truth of which there is no reason to doubt— recorded in letter cxlvii. where the deacon Sabinianus is charged with the attempted rape of a nun in the very cave of the Lord's Nativity at Bethlehem. Men were seeking Holy Orders " ut mulieres licentius videant " (xxii. 28). Most serious of all such offences was the scandal of the " Subintroductae " referred to in xxii. 14, and in cxvii. 9. These were women, not infrequently the Church's consecrated virgins, who, under the plea of spiritual sisterhood, resided with clergy, occupying not only the same house, but often the same sleeping chamber. It was an evil which early crept into the Church, for it is mentioned in the " Shepherd of Hermas " (Lib. iii. ; Simil. ix. 11), and continued both in East and West in spite of the decrees of Council after Council. On his appointment to Constantinople, Chrysostom found the practice firmly rooted, and his stern determination to suppress it was not the least potent cause of his banishment. There was, therefore, some justification for Jerome's strong language in xxii. 14 :

"How comes this plague of the Agapetae in the Church ? Whence come these unwedded wives or rather this new class of concubine—these harlots— for so I will call them, though they are the mistresses of but one man ? One house holds them and one room, often even one bed, yet they call us suspicious if we suppose that anything is amiss . . . both profess to have but one purpose, viz. to find spiritual consolation from a stranger; but their real aim is carnal intercourse."

Letter cxvii. to a mother and daughter living in Gaul is a flagrant example of women taking to themselves clerical protectors and paramours, and a vivid commentary on xxii. 14. It endorses the remarks of Sir Samuel Dill on p. 136 of his work :

"It would seem that the Church in conquering the citadel of the Empire had lost the freshness and purity of its early days. It had vanquished the external power of heathenism, it had still to subdue the forces of corruption within its own pale. The triumphant Church which has brought paganism to its knees, is very different from the Church of the Catacombs and persecutions."

Yet on Jerome's own showing, not all the clergy

THE CLERGY

were in a state of demoralisation. Writing to Rusticus he says: "the clergy are holy men and their lives are always worthy of praise" (cxxv.). He commends Exuperius, Bishop of Toulouse, as a model prelate, an imitator of the widow of Sarepta—self-denying, abstemious, generous; Nepotian he describes as a pattern priest, especially in his loving care of the sanctuary and its fittings—" sollicitus si niteret altare, si parietes absque fuligine, si pavimenta tersa, si janitor creber in porta, vela semper in ostiis, si sacrarium mundum, si vasa luculenta " (lx. 12).

Again, in letters vi. and vii. he mentions a certain deacon, Julian of Antioch, who had restored Jerome's sister to a virtuous life.

Not *all* the clergy, therefore, were given over to worldliness and greed. Were the allegations of avarice true on any large scale it would be difficult to account for the popularity of the ecclesiastical as compared with the civil courts and for the confidence generally felt in their justice. The fact that Ambrose and Augustine both complain of the heavy burden of their judicial duties is a sign that the people had not lost their respect for their pastors. In Rome, it is true, the splendour of the Papacy evokes the scorn of Ammianus Marcellinus, who describes Damasus supported by the offerings of matrons, driving out smartly dressed in a gorgeous carriage, and giving dinners which outrivalled those of the Emperor. It is a criticism which finds its counterpart in the " Farewell Oration " of Gregory Nazianzen to the Church of Constantinople :

" I did not know that we bishops were expected

to emulate the consuls, governors, and generals . . . to ride splendid horses, drive in magnificent carriages and be preceded by a procession, and surrounded by applause, and have every one make way for us as if we were wild beasts."

Yet the same Marcellinus goes on to say in effect that this state of affairs only prevailed in the capital cities. Some, at any rate, of the provincial prelates are earnestly commended by him for their modest demeanour, their abstemiousness, their humble apparel, and their downcast looks—in such marked contrast to the Roman pontiffs:

(" Qui esse poterant beati revera, si magnitudine urbis despecta, quam vitiis opponunt, ad imitationem antistitum quorundam provincialium viverent; quos tenuitas edendi potandique parcissime, vilitas etiam indumentorum, et supercilia humum spectantia, perpetuo numini verisque ejus cultoribus ut puros commendant et verecundos.")

Still on the whole, in spite of such evidence as the above, the general impression left on the mind by Jerome's " Mirror of the Clergy " is that, as far as the great cities are concerned, there had been distinct deterioration in the moral standards of the ministry.

(b) ORDERS

On the subject of the Orders of the Ministry there are in these epistles some significant side-lights. The three grades—bishops, priests, deacons, are everywhere in evidence, and Jerome, following the lead of Ambrosiaster, more than once compares them with the High Priest, priests and Levites of the

Old Covenant, *e.g.* cxlvi. 2, " quod Aaron et filii ejus atque Levitae in Templo fuerunt, hoc sibi episcopi et presbyteri et diaconi vindicent in ecclesia." Similarly in lii. 7, " quod Aaron et filios ejus, hoc esse episcopum et presbyteros noverimus."

Perhaps *the position of deacons* is not the least interesting point on which these letters throw light. From cxlvi. it seems that some contemporary of Jerome had taught that the diaconate was above the presbyterate (" audio quemdam in tantam erupisse vecordiam ut Diaconos Presbyteris, id est Episcopis anteferret "). At Rome, apparently, a presbyter could only be ordained on the recommendation of a deacon (" sed dices quomodo Romae ad testimonium Diaconi, Presbyter ordinatur ? "). Their pay, too, was higher than that of the priesthood, probably because of the fewness * of their numbers. Jerome had even seen a deacon seat himself among the presbyters in church and actually give his blessing to them at social gatherings. The indictment is confirmed by other evidence. The Council of Arles in 314 directs the deacons of the City of Rome not to take so much on themselves, but to defer to presbyters and act only on their sanction. The Council of Nicaea in 325 in its eighteenth Canon repeats this rebuke only without reference to Rome, an omission which suggests that the practices complained of had become more general, viz. administering the Eucharist to priests, receiving it before the bishops, and sitting down among presbyters in church. Jerome seems in this epistle cxlvi. to be borrowing the arguments of Ambrosiaster in the first of his " quaestiones "

* Sozomen, H. E. vii. 19, says that there were only seven in Rome.

where he treats of " de jactantia Romanorum levitarum." But the exaltation of the Diaconate to which they both refer was part of an upward movement in the ministry which marked the fourth and fifth centuries.

Presbyters were asserting a greater and greater independence of bishops; deacons were encroaching on the position of the presbyters, and sub-deacons on the sphere of deacons.

Mr. Turner (in the " Cambridge Mediaeval History," vol. i. pp. 154–5) thinks that the various protests against the arrogance of deacons were not without effect, for three deacon candidates, Felix, Ursinus, Eulalius, failed to secure election to the Papal throne.

But while these epistles recognise the threefold ministry as everywhere the rule in the Christian Church of the time, they insist no less clearly on the original identity of the two higher orders, *e.g.* lviii. 5: " let *bishops and presbyters* take for their examples the apostles . . . and *as they hold the rank which these once held*, let them endeavour to show the same excellence." Again, in lxix. 3 : " With the ancients these names (bishops and presbyters) were synonymous, one having reference to the office, the other to the age of the minister."

Similarly in cxlvi. 2 : " Of the names presbyter and bishop, the first denotes age, the second, rank," and, in the same passage, " in episcopo et presbyter continetur." This doctrine laid down so often by Jerome was, as Bishop Lightfoot says (commentary on Philippians, p. 99), " accepted without question by bishops and popes in succeeding ages." It is

THE CLERGY

noticeable that Pope Innocent in cxxxv. speaks of Jerome as "compresbyter," and that Augustine when Bishop of Hippo three times addresses him in the same way (lvi., lxvii., civ.). The later distinction between the two offices is accounted for as follows in letter cxlvi. 1 : * "When subsequently one presbyter was chosen to preside over the rest, this was done to remedy schism and to prevent each individual from rending the Church of Christ by drawing it to himself." Lightfoot in the above-named work (p. 230), says that the teaching of Jerome and Augustine on this point testifies to

" a substantial identity of order. Nor does it appear that this view was ever questioned until the era of the Reformation. In the Western Church at all events, it carried the sanction of the highest ecclesiastical authorities."

Very interesting but hopelessly difficult is St. Jerome's description of the Alexandrian ministry.

" For even at Alexandria from the time of Mark the Evangelist until the episcopates of Heraclas (A.D. 233–49) and Dionysius (A.D. 249–65), the presbyters always nominated as bishop one chosen out of their own body and placed in a higher grade, just as an army elects a general, or as deacons appoint one of themselves whom they know to be diligent and call him Archdeacon." †

The meaning of the words has been keenly

* A similar statement occurs in his commentary on Titus i. 5.
† " Nam et Alexandriae a Marco Evangelista usque ad Heraclam et Dionysium episcopos, presbyteri semper unum ex se electum, in excelsiori gradu collocatum, episcopum nominabant : quomodo si exercitus imperatorem faciat : aut diaconi elegant de se quem industrium noverint et Archidiaconum vocent " (cxlvi. 1).

14 THE EPISTLES OF ST. JEROME

disputed and the best authorities are in complete disagreement as to the exact interpretation of the passage. Lightfoot ("Commentary on Philippians," p. 231) says: "Though the direct statement of this father refers only to the *appointment* of the bishop, still it may be inferred that the function of the presbyters extended also to the *consecration*."

This view receives the weighty support of Bishop John Wordsworth who in his "Ministry of Grace," pp. 135 ff., endorses the opinion of Morinus that the judgment of Hilary the deacon was correct on 1 Tim. iii. 8: "Episcopi et Presbyteri una ordinatio est." "Doubtful," says Wordsworth, "as it may be as a statement of general application, I believe that Morinus is right as regards Rome and Alexandria up to the beginning or middle of the third century." He (Wordsworth) thinks that Jerome got his information about Alexandria from Epiphanius, Bishop of Salamis, who knew Egypt well.

Dr. Bigg in his "Origins of Christianity," p. 121, agrees with the view of Lightfoot and Wordsworth.

On the other hand, Bingham ("Antiquities," Book II., ciii. 5) believes that Jerome is only speaking of the *choice* not the *consecration* of the bishop, and contends that the words in letter cxlvi., "Quid enim facit *excepta ordinatione* episcopus quod presbyter non faciat?" imply that some higher authority confirmed the act of the presbyters.

Bishop Gore in his "Church and Ministry," pp. 137 ff., maintains that Jerome, wishing to denounce the arrogance of deacons, emphasises as a corrective the dignity of that priesthood which, with some differences of function, presbyter and bishop share in common.

THE CLERGY

" It requires a great effort of confidence to trust Jerome's witness, especially when we consider it is the witness of Jerome in a temper and that under such circumstances he is not too careful with his facts " (*ibid.* 142).

But even if true, the statement in cxlvi. is not inconsistent with the principle of succession, it would simply mean that at Alexandria there was only one ordination which made a man both a presbyter and also a potential bishop (p. 143). Gore quotes against Jerome Hadrian's letter to Servianus in A.D. 130 in which he (Hadrian) declares that he saw at Alexandria those who call themselves bishops of Christ, but no presbyter, " nemo Christianorum presbyter."

Whether we have regard to the weight of authority on either side or to the actual words of Jerome— generally so lucid, here unfortunately so ambiguous— a definite conclusion seems equally impossible, and " not proven " the only verdict. Jerome's illustrations suggest superficially that some higher authority ratified and completed the choice of the presbyters. Normally the Senate would confirm the Army's nominee and invariably a new archdeacon would require the sanction and approval of the bishop. Nor when Jerome asks " quid facit excepta ordinatione episcopus quod presbyter non faciat ? " does there seem any doubt that in his opinion no presbyter could ordain; yet there are considerations which lead to a different decision. There is evidence, direct and indirect, that the appointment of the bishop did not follow the course which normally prevailed elsewhere.

(1) Alexandria was a university town where

16 THE EPISTLES OF ST. JEROME

Christians did not hesitate to attend the lectures of pagan professors. In such a cosmopolitan centre, the headquarters of Neo-Platonism, where the atmosphere was predominantly intellectual, it would hardly be a matter of surprise if the government of the Church developed on somewhat independent and unusual lines.

(2) The parochial system, which was no part of the Roman Church organisation even at the end of the fifth century, is known to have been in full operation at Alexandria in the third. It was his position as parish priest of Baucalis which was one of the principal factors in propagating the heresy of Arius. This early development of the parochial system at Alexandria seems to point to a special importance attaching to presbyters.

(3) The ultimate failure of the presbyter Arius and the victory of the Bishop Alexander, may, as Mr. Turner remarks in the "Cambridge Mediaeval History," vol i. pp. 159–60, have depressed the status of the Alexandrian presbyters generally, who were forbidden to preach there after the Arian trouble.

(4) There is the story that the hermit Poemen was visited one day by heretics, who abused the Archbishop of Alexandria as having only presbyterian ordination (ὥς ὅτι παρὰ πρεσβυτέρων ἔχοι τὴν χειροτονίαν). The story must represent a local tradition of the latter half of the fourth century.

(5) Dr. Kidd in his "History of the Church to A.D. 461," vol. i. pp. 381–2, refers to the well-known turbulence of the Alexandrian mob, and suggests that for the avoidance of tumult the powers which elsewhere belonged to the *people* were transferred to a college

THE CLERGY 17

of presbyters (but it is possible that the unusual powers of the presbyterate were those elsewhere exercised by the episcopate).

(6) Severus, monophysite patriarch of Antioch, writing somewhere between 518 and 538, in Egypt, and recording local tradition, declares that "the bishop of the city of the Alexandrians used in former days to be appointed by the presbyters."

(7) There is the statement of Eutychius in the tenth century that by an ordinance of St. Mark, the presbyters of Alexandria were to elect one of their own number as patriarch. This testimony, however, is too late to be trustworthy.

(8) Irregular ordinations were not unknown in the early Church. Besides the notorious instance of Paphnutius, there is the case of Ambrose made Bishop of Milan when an unbaptised layman, and of Cyprian who was ordained priest without having first been a deacon. Jerome in lxix. 9 protests against the practice of ordaining novices : " heri catechumenus, hodie pontifex; heri in amphitheatro, hodie in ecclesia; vespere in circo, mane in altario; dudum fautor histrionum, nunc virginum consecrator."

At one period, even, a confessor might become a priest without any ordination (see the Canons of Hippolytus, vi. 43–7 : " immo confessio est, ordinatio ejus ").

Alexandria may well be, therefore, yet another departure from what afterwards became the universal practice and fixed tradition of the Christian Church.

Yet, on the other hand, it must be remembered :

(1) That a section which may be dated *c.* 200–230 of the Egyptian Document, called " The Apostolic

18   THE EPISTLES OF ST. JEROME

Church Order," shows clearly enough that there were bishops in Egypt in the early third century, and provides rules for their election even where there are not twelve voters.

(2) Origen when deposed from the priesthood by a synod of bishops at the instance of Demetrius, never protests against their action as a novel and unconstitutional assumption of authority.

(3) The charge against Athanasius of having been ordained by presbyters, may be, as Mr. Turner surmises:

" one line of the Arian campaign against him. They wished to turn the edge of any argument that might be based on the solidarity of the episcopate. If the Catholics called upon the bishops of the East not to champion a rebellious presbyter, their opponents would answer on this view that Athanasius was no more than a presbyter himself. . . . Jerome writing amid Syrian surroundings would eagerly accept the there current presentation of the Alexandrian tradition, though his knowledge of the later facts caused him to throw back the dates from the known to the unknown, from Athanasius and Alexander to Dionysius and Heraclas " (" Cambridge Mediaeval History," vol. i. pp. 160–1).

Forced and semi-forced ordinations are still a feature of Church life in the fourth and fifth centuries. Jerome's own case nearly but not quite comes under this description. Writing to Pammachius against John of Jerusalem (section 41) he quotes his own words to Bishop Paulinus of Antioch and shows that his ordination was scarcely of his own seeking. " Did I ask to be ordained by you ? If, in bestowing the

THE CLERGY

rank of presbyter, you do not strip us of the monastic state, you can bestow or withhold ordination as you think best."

In li. 1 Epiphanius relates how Jerome's brother, Paulinian, had several times fled from John of Jerusalem in order to avoid the onerous duties of the priesthood, and tells how he himself (Epiphanius) had deputed a number of deacons to seize him and stop his mouth while he forced him into the ministry. Perhaps, under such circumstances, it is scarcely strange that there were in the Church presbyters who, like Jerome and Vincent, rarely or never actively exercised their office.

As to the choice of ordinands, it seems from cxxv. 17 that it rested sometimes with the bishop, sometimes with the people " cum ad perfectam aetatem veneris, si tamen vita comes fuerit, et te vel populus, vel Pontifex civitatis, in clericum elegerit."

II

SCRIPTURE STUDY

THE VULGATE

IF diligent searching of the Scriptures be a sign of spiritual health, the Church of St. Jerome's day was indeed in a state of sound and vigorous vitality.

The one hundred and fifty letters in Migne's twenty-second volume reveal, in every quarter of the Christian world, evidence of careful, devout, and even critical study of the Bible both by clergy and laity. The well-known " cucurbita " story in epistles civ. and cxii. shows with what interest and closeness of attention the laity followed the lessons in the *public services* of the Church. But that the same spirit possessed them in their *private* reading at home there is stronger testimony still.

The monks of the Egyptian desert learn every day passages of it by heart : " Quotidie aliquid de Scripturis discitur " (lii. 5).

Paula's virgins do the same : " non licebat cuiquam sororum ignorare psalmos et non de Scripturis quotidie aliquid discere " (cviii. 19). Bishop *Damasus* himself is a keen student both of the Old and New Testaments and repeatedly writes to Jerome on such points as the meaning of " Hosanna " (xix.), the

SCRIPTURE STUDY

interpretation of Isaiah's vision (xviii.), the true exposition of the parable of the Prodigal Son (xxi.), and of such passages as Gen. iv. 15; Acts x. 15; Gen. xxvii., etc. (xxxv.).

Marcella, the head of a religious society in Rome, delighted in the Scriptures to an incredible degree: " divinarum Scripturarum ardor erat incredibilis " (cxxvii. 4). She seeks from Jerome an explanation of such terms as " Alleluia," " Selah," " Amen," " sin against the Holy Ghost "; the twelve Hebrew names for God: " Ephod," " Teraphim " (letters xxv., xxvi., xxviii.). She further inquires of him what are the " things which eye hath not seen nor ear heard," 1 Cor. ii. 9, and whether the " sheep " and the " goats " in St. Matthew xxv. are or are not Christians and heathens respectively. She would also like to know the exact significance of 1 Thess. iv. 15–17, of St. Matthew xxviii. 9, when compared with St. John xx. 17, and whether our Lord before His Ascension was both in heaven and on earth (lix.). As a help to her biblical studies, she requests Jerome to lend her Rhetitius' Commentary on the Song of Songs (xxxvii.).

Fabiola, another Roman lady, is, if possible, more zealous still in the same direction: " et veluti quamdam famen satiare desiderans, per Prophetas Evangelia, Psalmosque currebat, quaestiones et proponens et solutas recondens in scriniŏlo pectoris sui " (lxxvii. 7). She even asked and obtained from Jerome an exhaustive exposition of the forty-two halting-places of the children of Israel at the exodus from Egypt (lxxviii.).

Paula knew the Scriptures by heart and could

chant the Psalms in Hebrew (cviii. 26, Migne). "Scripturas sanctas tenebat memoriter . . . Hebraeam linguam discere voluit et consecuta est ut Psalmos Hebraice caneret." In another letter, liv. 13, he writes to Furia of the same matron : " O si videres sororem tuam . . . audires totam veteris et Novi Testamenti supellectilem ex illius corde fervere." To another woman, the virgin *Principia*, Jerome sends, at her request, a detailed explanation of Psalm xlv., " eructavit cor meum " (lxv.). In cvi. he expresses his joy that even *among the Getae* are diligent students of the Scriptures like Sunnias and Fretela who send him a long list of questions as to the differences between the Septuagint and Jerome's Latin Psalter of A.D. 383. Similarly *in Gaul* are two ladies, *Hedibia* and *Algasia*, who between them submit to him for solution no less than twenty-three Scriptural problems (cxx., cxxi.).

Blesilla, in a few months, or rather days, so completely mastered the difficulties of Hebrew as to emulate her mother's (Paula's) zeal in learning and singing psalms : "in paucis non dicam mensibus sed diebus Hebraeae linguae vicerat difficultates ut in discendis canendisque Psalmis cum matre contenderet " (xxxix. 1). Again in lxxv. 4, *Lucinius*, a wealthy *Spaniard*, is praised for his keenness and diligence in sacred study : " ego in illo magis laudabo fervorem et studium Scripturarum." In cxl., *Cyprian*, a presbyter, receives from Jerome an exposition of Psalm xc. and in cxix. two monks of *Toulouse*, *Minervius* and *Alexander*, obtain from him answers to their questions about 1. Cor. xv. 51 and 1 Thess. iv. 17. In cxxxix. he replies at some length to inquiries by

SCRIPTURE STUDY

Dardanus, prefect of Gaul, as to "quae sit terra repromissionis." Even the great *St. Augustine* consults him as to the meaning of St. James ii. 10, and the exact interpretation of the quarrel between St. Peter and St. Paul at Antioch—a quarrel which Jerome regarded not as real but as a wholly fictitious dispute intended to impress on Christians the mischief of conforming to the Mosaic Law (lvi.). In lxxiii. he (Jerome) suggests to *Evangelus* that Melchizedek was a real human being, probably Shem, the eldest son of Noah.

In lxxiv., he tells *Rufinus*, a Roman presbyter, that the judgment of Solomon in 1 Kings iii. is a parable and that the true and false mothers are types respectively of the Church and the Synagogue.

Whatever may be thought of the soundness or otherwise of his interpretations, such as those of 1 Kings iii. and of the dispute at Antioch, it is none the less clear from the foregoing and many similar passages in St. Jerome's epistles, that throughout the length and breadth of Christendom, not only women but men—laymen as well as clergy—were giving minute and earnest attention to the study of the Bible. And when it is remembered that every copy of a book was at this time made by hand, at no small expenditure of time and money, the extent and profundity of these studies are remarkable indeed. The Church could never be regarded as moribund while such a condition of things continued. In the encouragement and impetus he gave to sacred learning, St. Jerome is seen to best advantage. As a director of devotees he is in ceaseless request. His patience with his pupils and correspondents seems tireless and illimitable. No pains are too great for him to take on their behalf, no research is too laborious. Whatever the tax on his time and thought, he pays it willingly to the uttermost farthing. He is the Gamaliel at whose feet all sorts of disciples proudly gather, nor does he send a single inquirer empty away. Their interests he identifies with his own, and not even sickness or barbarian invasions, still less his own private business are suffered to divert him for long from this labour of love. Probably he occupies, in this respect, an unique position which has never been quite paralleled before or since in the long history of the Catholic Church. He had in a special degree the faculty of kindling in his converts and scholars the true love of learning, inspiring them with his own infectious enthusiasm for Christian truth. He had also the gift, rare even in professed teachers, of lucidity in imparting knowledge. Perhaps the man who approached most nearly to him " longo sed proximus intervallo," was the Venerable Bede, whose whole life, like Jerome's, was spent in learning, teaching, and writing. Origen, the greatest of Christian teachers, is his closest counterpart in earlier times.

There was, however, one serious difficulty in the path both of the instructor and the instructed, and that was the state both of the Greek and Latin *

---

* " The oldest Latin version had been made not later than the second century in Africa, the Old Testament portion being from the Septuagint. It is called 'the African Latin.'

" A second, sufficiently different to be, in all probability, independent, was in use in North Italy in Jerome's time, and has a type of text known as 'the European Latin.' Successive revisions of this, whether casual or systematic, produced after *c*. 350, a third type of text called 'the Italian Latin.'

"These three types are classed together under the common name of

SCRIPTURE STUDY 25

Biblical texts, but especially of the latter. Most of the evidence is, strictly, outside the scope of this work, being found in the "Prefaces" and the more formal treatises of St. Jerome, but passing allusions to some of the passages may be permitted, as they are necessary to any adequate discussion of the textual criticism of the time.

(1) *With regard to the Septuagint.*—Students like Sunnias and Fretela in cvi. 2, were greatly exercised by the frequent discrepancies between Jerome's so-called Roman Psalter and their own copy of the Septuagint. In reply Jerome explains that they are using the common "Vulgata" and untrustworthy text which differed widely from the critical text of Origen as given in the Hexapla and used by himself: "Κοινὴ . . . vetus corrupta editio est. Ea autem quae habetur in ʽΕξαπλοῖς et quam nos vertimus, ipsa est quae in eruditorum libris incorrupta et immaculata Septuaginta Interpretum translatio reservatur" (cvi. 2).

In his "Preface" to the "Book of Hebrew Questions," Jerome says that one of his aims is to correct the FAULTS which *teem* in the Greek and Latin copies of the Hebrew Scriptures; that he has found the Septuagint most accurate in the Pentateuch, which alone, according to Josephus, was the work of the seventy translators; that it (the Septuagint) omits various Old Testament passages quoted in the New Testament, especially those of Messianic import out of deference to Ptolemy and his anxiety

the 'Old Latin Version.' Jerome was to take various manuscripts of this version, and bring the text into agreement with the Greek. He felt that it was a heavy task." (Kidd, "A History of the Church," vol. ii. p. 824.)

not to hurt Jewish prejudices; also that the best MSS. are those which correspond most closely with the quotations in the New Testament.

In the " Preface to Daniel," he states that as far as that book is concerned, the Church had discarded the Septuagint entirely, and had substituted for it the version of Theodotion.

In his translation from the Greek of the books of Chronicles, he says in his " Preface " to the work, that the MSS. of the Septuagint in the matter of Hebrew names of places were so corrupt that occasionally three names were run into one, and " you would think that you had before you, not a heap of Hebrew names, but those of some foreign and Sarmatian tribe."

(2) But if the state of the *Greek* MSS. of the Old Testament were bad, that of the *Latin* MSS. was infinitely worse. In xxvii. 1, writing to Marcella, he speaks of "Latinorum codicum vitiositatem." In section (3) of the same epistle, he gives instances of careless copying, *e.g.* Romans xii. 11, 12 : " tempori (Καιρῷ) servientes " for " Domino (Κυρίῳ) servientes "; also 1 Tim. v. 19, where the qualifying phrase was omitted "nisi sub duobus aut tribus testibus "; also 1 Tim. i. 15 and iii. 1, where " humanus sermo " was substituted for " fidelis sermo."

In xviii. 21, he complains " in Latinis codicibus propter interpretum varietatem." In all these statements he is confirmed by his contemporary, St. Augustine, who says (De Doct. Christ ii. 11): " Qui Scripturas ex Hebraea lingua in Graecam verterunt numerari possunt, Latini autem interpretes nullo modo."

Later in the same passage he speaks of " Infinita varietas Latinorum interpretum." And in letter civ. 6—writing to Jerome—he remarks what a very useful service the latter would be rendering if he would translate into accurate Latin those Greek Scriptures which were the handiwork of the Seventy— for the existing Latin versions of them varied so much in different MSS. as to be altogether intolerable and were so strongly suspected of containing what was not in the Greek that people hesitated to use them for argument or proof. Some of the variants were due to careless copying, others to deliberate falsification for doctrinal reasons, *e.g.* in Adv. Jovinian i. 13, he complains that in 1 Cor. vii. 35, " πρὸς τὸ εὔσχημον καὶ εὐπρόσεδρον τῷ Κυρίῳ ἀπερισπάστως " are wanting in the Latin MSS.; and in (26) of the same work that the text in 1 Cor. ix. 5 had been tampered with both by the advocates and opponents of celibacy—ἀδελφήν or ἀδελφάς, having been added in later MSS. to the original γυναῖκας.

Similarly in Adv. Vigilantium (6) with regard to 2 Esdras vii. 35 : " after death no one dares to pray for others "—the passage occurs in the Arabic and Ethiopic versions, but not in the Latin, being rejected probably for dogmatic considerations. Something like this was the textual state of affairs, when Damasus, realising the chaos which existed, commissioned Jerome to revise the Old Latin Versions of the New Testament. The work could not have been placed in better hands.

" Jerome's qualifications were unique : he was fully sensible of the urgency and importance of such a revision ; he was a good Latin scholar, writing a style that was pure and vigorous; he had been studying Greek carefully and had already a fair knowledge of Hebrew; in later years, when he was translating the Old Testament from the original, he had attained a thorough knowledge of that language, while long residence and travel in the East had given him that firsthand acquaintance with the country and its customs which must be invaluable to anyone undertaking a task of this nature. His ability, also, as a scholar and writer were well known; and Damasus must have argued that a version proceeding from an authority so eminent and backed by the influence and power of the Roman see, could not fail to obtain a wide acceptance." (H. J. White, Article "Vulgate" in Hastings' "Dictionary of the Bible," p. 874.)

The need and the nature of the commission given to Jerome are best seen in the letter prefixed by Wordsworth and White to their edition of the Vulgate Gospels, the substance of which is as follows :

" Jerome to the blessed Pope Damasus "—" You bid me undertake a new work out of an old one, viz. that among the copies of the Scriptures scattered over the whole world I should take my seat as a sort of umpire, and *inasmuch as they differ from each other*, that I should decide which of them are in agreement with the correct Greek original. A holy task! but a piece of presumption on my part full of peril to myself; " . . . " for if any reliance is to be placed on the Latin copies, let them tell us on which of them— for they are almost as numerous as the MSS. If, however, the truth is to be sought from several, why should we not go back to the Greek source and correct those which have either been *badly edited by faulty interpreters*, or even more *wrongly emended by pre-*

sumptuous and *unskilful persons*, or *added to or altered by sleepy transcribers.*"

To much the same effect is his letter to Marcella (xxvii. 1) where, defending himself against charges of tampering with the text, he says: " The Latin MSS. of the Scriptures are proved to be *faulty by the variations which all of them exhibit*, and my aim has been to restore them to the form of the Greek original."

So far as the New Testament is concerned, it seems that Jerome in his version generally preferred to follow (1) a MS. very like the Sinaitic, and (2) another which Wordsworth and White were unable to identify. In their second volume dealing with the Acts of the Apostles, p. 10, they say: " Scripsimus in Epilogo ad Evangelia (i. p. 660) Hieronymum nostro judicio tum textus formam cum Sinaitico codice plus minus concordantem cognovisse, tum alteram valde alienam quae nobis alias ignota sit," et (p. 662) " Hieronymum ad manus habuisse codices Graecos qui ab omnibus qui ad nos pervenerunt diversi fuerint." " Nobis tamen hanc sententiam confirmavit investigatio textus Actuum Apostolorum " (vol. ii. p. 11).

As to the Old Testament, Jerome seems to have had much less difficulty, following an unpointed Hebrew text substantially identical with the Massoretic. Possibly the Rabbi Akiba had simplified his task by destroying in his ultra-patriotic zeal all texts of the Hebrew Old Testament which were not of proved *Palestinian origin.*

In this work of revision and translation Jerome had to face many other difficulties besides the bewildering variant readings of the versions. The ingrained conservatism which is opposed to everything but that which is familiar, the mental inertia which clings to the accustomed even at the expense of truth, are well illustrated in letters civ. 5 and cxii. 22; Jerome, in Jonah iv. 6, had rendered the Hebrew word קִיקָיוֹן by "*hedera*," whereas the old Latin had had "*cucurbita*." The introduction of the new word into Divine Service was so deeply resented by the congregation and was the cause of so much commotion, that the bishop of a certain town in Africa was, in consequence, left almost entirely without a flock:

"Factus est tantus tumultus in plebe, maxime Graecis arguentibus, et inflammantibus calumniam falsitatis, ut cogeretur Episcopus . . . Judaeorum testimonium flagitare . . . quid plura? Coactus est homo velut mendositatem corrigere, volens, post magnum periculum, non remanere sine plebe" (civ. 5).

In cxii. 22, Jerome again refers to this incident: "Dicis me in Jonam Prophetam male quiddam interpretatum, et seditione populi conclamante propter unius verbi dissonantiam, Episcopum pene Sacerdotium perdidisse" (cxii. 22).

M. Thierry ("Saint Jerome," livre xi. pp. 447-8, 4th ed.) doubts if the incident ever actually occurred, but both Jerome and Augustine, who had the best means of knowing, speak of it as a fact. Indeed, it is more probable that it is in some respects typical of the hostile reception accorded to the Vulgate in the early days of its history, before its merits and its superiority to other versions had won general acknowledgment.

Another obstacle in Jerome's path was the almost superstitious sanctity with which the Septuagint was now regarded. Even Augustine held it to be equally inspired with the original Hebrew, and gives frank expression to his feelings on the subject in his " de Civitate Dei," Book XVIII. Chapter 43. There he tells his readers that there have been indeed *other* interpreters who have translated the Hebrew scriptures into Greek, *e.g.* Aquila, Symmachus, Theodotion, and the author of the " Quinta "; but it is the Septuagint which has been received by the Church as the only one, so much so that many Christians were quite unaware of the existence of any other versions. *Latin* translations of the Septuagint were indeed in vogue among the Latin Churches, and quite recently the presbyter Jerome, a most learned man and well versed in all three languages, had turned the Scriptures directly from the Hebrew into Latin—yet, though the Jews declared his work correct and said the Septuagint was often at fault, the Churches of Christ rightly insist that when seventy learned men had produced a version and agreed upon certain readings, no single translator could be suffered to take precedence of them. " Spiritus enim qui in Prophetis erat, quando illa dixerunt, idem ipse erat in Septuaginta viris, quando illa interpretati sunt." And even though it was true that certain passages in the Greek were not to be found in the Hebrew, that fact was no ground for their rejection. Whatever was in the Hebrew and not in the Greek was to be understood in this way, namely, that the Spirit of God had some special reason for wishing Jews and not Greeks to say it; and, similarly, whatever occurs in the Septuagint and not in the Hebrew He preferred should be said by the one and not by the other, thus showing that both parties were prophets.

Echoes of this teaching occur in his letters to Jerome, *e.g.* in lvi. 2 (Migne, vol. xxii.), in which he urges him to adhere in future more closely to the text of the Septuagint " *quorum est gravissima auctoritas.*" Similarly in civ. 4, " ego sane te mallem Graecas potius canonicas nobis interpretari Scripturas quae Septuaginta Interpretum auctoritate perhibentur."

A third difficulty was his comparatively slender knowledge of Hebrew at the outset of his task, a difficulty, however, which vanished as time went on. In days when there were no written grammars or lexicons of the language, he was dependent entirely on oral teaching from Jews. He began in the desert of Chalcis and continued and perfected it at Bethlehem at great trouble and expense, a Jew named Baraninas coming to him, he says, like a second Nicodemus by night : " Quo labore ! quo pretio ! Baraninam habui praeceptorem " (lxxxiv. 3).

Altogether, Jerome was engaged in the work of Biblical revision and translation for upwards of twenty years (A.D. 385-405), and as he proceeded it became more and more evident to him that the only permanent and satisfactory solution of the problem confronting him was a new translation made direct from the original Hebrew of the Old Testament and the original Greek of the New. Over and over again in his letters he gives expression to this ever deepening conviction, and the suggestive phrase " Hebraica veritas " tersely summarises his sentiments. It is in the " Prefaces " that his strongest sayings on the

SCRIPTURE STUDY

subject are to be found, but the epistles also, in scarcely slighter degree, witness to this—his fundamental principle; *e.g.* in xxviii. 5 he writes to Marcella, "this have we quaffed from the innermost fountain of the Hebrews, not following the streamlets of opinions and errors of which the whole world is full." Similarly in xx. 2, " it remains therefore to ignore the streamlets of opinions and go back to the fountain "; or again in lxxi. 5 : " The New Testament I have restored to the authoritative form of the Greek original. For as the true text of the Old Testament can only be tested by a reference to the Hebrew, so the true text of the New requires for its decision an appeal to the Greek." In cvi. 2 he insists to Sunnias and Fretela that as in the case of the New Testament, when there are variants in the Latin copies—recourse is had to the original Greek, so in the case of the Old, when there are differences in the Greek and Latin versions we betake ourselves to the Hebrew truth."

A second principle to which Jerome firmly adhered was to carefully differentiate between the canonical Scriptures and the Apocrypha. In cvii. 12 Laeta is directed to see that the younger Paula avoids apocryphal books, and that if she should read them she should understand that many faulty elements have crept into them and that considerable discretion is required in looking for gold in the midst of dirt. But it is in the " Prefaces " where he is most emphatic as to the distinction, particularly in those to Proverbs and to his translation from the Septuagint of the Books of Solomon. In the former he says :

" As then the Church reads Judith, Tobit, and the books of Maccabees, but does not admit them among the canonical Scriptures, let it read these two volumes (Wisdom and Ecclesiasticus) for the edification of the people, not to give authority to the doctrines of the Church."

A third principle by which Jerome was guided in his translation was to give the reader the *sense*, rather than a literal rendering of the original. In lvii. 5 he applies to his own case the rule which, he says, all the best translators in secular literature have followed, namely, " non verbum e verbo sed sensum exprimere de sensu " ; a rule to which he adhered more or less consistently, in spite of his disclaimer in the same passage where he says that in Holy Scripture " even the order of the words is a mystery, manifold meanings lie hidden in each single word " (" et verborum ordo mysterium est, in verbis singulis multiplices latent intelligentiae "). In section 10 of the same work he remarks " non verba in Scripturis consideranda sed sensus," *i.e.* " in dealing with the Scriptures it is the sense one must look to and not the words " ; a principle on which, generally speaking, he did not fail to act, as the following examples show : (1) being an example of drastic compression, (2) of amplification, (3) of interpretation.

(1) וַיַּעַל מֵעָלָיו אֱלֹהִים בַּמָּקוֹם אֲשֶׁר־דִּבֶּר אִתּוֹ׃

(="and God went up from him in the place where He spake with him ").

The Vulgate rendering is simply " Et recessit ab eo " (Genesis xxxv. 13).

(2) וְהַמַּחֲנֶה הָיָה בֶטַח׃

(=" the camp was secure ").

The Vulgate rendering is " castra *hostium* qui securi erant *et nihil adversi suspicabantur* " ; the italicised words having no equivalent in the original (Judges viii. 11).

(3) πρηνὴς γενόμενος ἐλάκησε μέσος.

Vulgate="Suspensus crepuit medius," where Jerome evidently suggests that Judas hung himself over some steep place, that the rope broke and that he was dashed to pieces (Acts i. 18).

It is an exaggerated claim which Jerome makes for his own work, when writing to Pammachius he says:

"I have lately translated Job into our mother tongue . . . read it both in Greek and in Latin and compare the old version with my translation. You will then clearly see that the difference between them is that between truth and falsehood " (xlix. 4).

Still, the Church owes an undying debt to him for the Vulgate Version and for the scholarly instincts which, in spite of St. Augustine and others, refused to look for guidance to anything but the earliest MSS. and the original languages of the Bible. Bishop Westcott well says:

"It can scarcely be denied that the Vulgate is not only the most venerable but also the most precious monument of Latin Christianity. For ten centuries it preserved in Western Europe a text of Holy Scripture far purer than that which was current in the Byzantine Church " (Smith, " Dictionary of the Bible," vol. iii. p. 1715; article " Vulgate ");

and on p. 1718 of the same volume : " it was the version which alone they knew who handed down to the Reformers the rich stores of mediaeval wisdom." Dean Milman points out how " it contributed to form the dialect of ecclesiastical Latin which became the religious language of Europe " (" History of Christianity," vol. iii. p. 352), and also in a footnote on the same page adds : * " There appears to me more of the Oriental character in the Old Testament of the Vulgate than in the LXX. That translation having been made by Greeks, or by Jews domiciled in a Greek city, the Hebrew style seems subdued, as far as possible, to the Greek. Jerome seems to have endeavoured to Hebraise or Orientalise his Latin." Grützmacher in the " Encyclopædia of Religion and Ethics," vol. vii., article " Jerome," says that while

" Jerome was no great creative spirit as was Augustine . . . he was certainly the most learned of the Latin Fathers. Not only was he equipped with an extensive knowledge of profane and sacred literature, but he surpassed all the Fathers in his mastery of Hebrew. *His significance lies in the fact that he stands supreme among those who mediated the religious heritage of Hebrew and Greek antiquity to the Latin world* " . . . " Jerome's translation of the Bible is a most praiseworthy achievement, inasmuch as, taken all in all, it maintains a sort of middle course between an extreme literality on the one hand and an extreme freedom on the other " (*ibid.*).

The translators of the so-called " authorised " version of 1611 pay him a noble tribute when they say :

" Again they were not out of the Hebrew fountain (we speak of the Latin translations of the Old Testa-

---

* *Cf.* Mr. Ruskin's panegyric of Jerome and the Vulgate in " Our Fathers have told us " (Chapter III. 37–8).

ment) but out of the Greek stream; therefore, the Greek being not altogether clear, the Latin derived from it must needs be muddy. This moved St. Hierome, a most learned Father, and the best linguist without controversy of his age or of any other which went before him, to undertake the translating of the Old Testament out of the very fountains themselves; which he performed with that evidence of great learning, judgment, industry, and faithfulness that he hath for ever bound the Church unto him in a debt of special remembrance and thankfulness " (" Translators to the reader ").

Letter cxxix. 3 witnesses incidentally to the hard struggle of two New Testament books to secure a place in the canon of Scripture. The Latin fathers, he says, did not recognise the Epistle to the Hebrews, while the Greek fathers rejected the Revelation of St. John. Jerome insists on the canonicity of each—of the former, because it is read in the daily lessons of the Church; of the latter, because it has the recognition of "ancient writers." (It was Montanist millenarian extravagances which had brought it into disfavour.)

III

THE ASCETIC AND MONASTIC MOVEMENT

NO study of Jerome would be complete which did not deal with the ascetic and monastic movement in which he was so conspicuous a figure.

Restraint, abstinence, self-discipline for the sake of the individual soul and of the Kingdom of Heaven, were duties clearly recognised in the gospels and acted upon by the first followers of our Lord. But for some considerable time after the introduction of Christianity, no one seems to have felt any call to withdraw from the world in order to put these principles into practice. Ordinary everyday life was regarded as sufficient field for their exercise, and to cut himself off from his fellow-creatures was a step which never seems to have suggested itself even to the strictest Christian. His fasts and prayers, his acts of charity and sacrifice were all done in private and in the seclusion of his own home. It was not till the Decian persecution of A.D. 250 that a more public and pronounced form of asceticism began to appear. Then hundreds of Christians in Egypt fled for safety to the desert, many of whom remained there permanently. Communities of women seem to have preceded those of men, for *c.* 250 Antony placed his sister in a

THE ASCETIC AND MONASTIC MOVEMENT 39

παρθενῶν—the first recorded instance of anything of the kind in Christian history. Antony himself may be regarded as the founder of Eastern Monachism, living, as he did, for fifteen years, a life of solitude near a town, and then withdrawing about 285 to a disused fort in the desert at Pispir by the Nile in strictest seclusion—only leaving it to take up in earnest the organisation of monachism for those who had settled near him by the Red Sea. To the mind of Antony, Christianity was ἄσκησις and nothing else, and his system, if such it can be called, was " go as you please," each ascetic being a law to himself. It was eremite or semi-eremite in character, most of the monks being solitaries, but some living in groups of twos and threes or even of greater numbers. Such manual labour as they wrought was slight and sedentary, e.g. basket making and linen-weaving, and was intended either as a penance or to kill time. They observed both Sabbath and Sunday as days of worship, assembling together in church, but on the other days saying their devotions in the privacy of their own cells. Scete, Cellia—a desert, and Nitria— sixty miles south of Alexandria, were its chief centres. Palladius, who visited them in 390, says there were 600 monks in Cellia and 5,000 in Nitria.

The next development is associated with the name of Pachomius (A.D. 292–346) whose ascetics lived by rule and whose system was coenobitic. Jerome says (Praef. in Reg. Pach., Migne xxiii. 96) that his organisation was of a quasi-military character and that the houses were arranged according to trades, fullers, e.g. in one, and carpenters in another. Manual work indeed—no less than prayer and the learning of

Scripture by heart—was an essential element of the Pachomian system and was obligatory on all the monks whatever their previous social rank. It was at its best when Palladius and Cassian came in contact with it at the end of the fourth century; deterioration set in with the fifth; most of the monks became Monophysites and presently were practically wiped out in the Mahomedan invasions.

Jerome reckons the number of Pachomian monks at 50,000, but Palladius' more sober and cautious estimate of 7,000 is probably much nearer the truth. His coenobitic system, as more fully developed by Basil, became the basis and model of Western Monachism. Basil not only made work a compulsory part of the curriculum but maintained its superiority to mere austerity. Thus he built orphanages and schools in which he made his monks teach the children.

But of both types, Antonian and Pachomian, it may be said that however exalted the original ideal of the founders might be, it was not long before decay began to appear. The danger point was reached when Monachism became a fashion and the monk succeeded to the place in public opinion once held by the martyr in the days of the persecutions. Dr. Kidd in his "History of the Church" (vol. ii. p. 104), remarks how the former took up "the title and rôle of an 'athlete,' only his 'agony' was self-imposed, and in his capacity of 'athlete' he tried to beat all records." He mentions in particular one Macarius of Alexandria " one of the celebrities of the cells," between Nitria and Scete, who could never hear of a feat of self-discipline without striving forthwith to surpass it. It needed the stern hand of

THE ASCETIC AND MONASTIC MOVEMENT 41

a St. Benedict to suppress these extravagances and prohibit what Dr. Kidd (*ibid.*) well calls "private venture in asceticism."

It was about A.D. 340 when Athanasius with two Egyptian anchorites came to Rome, and from that time for many years afterwards the movement gathered strength in the West alike from the quantity and quality of its converts. No one took it up with greater enthusiasm or preached it more persistently than Jerome, and it was mainly owing to his strenuous advocacy that it became rooted so deeply in Western Christendom. Yet he was by no means blind to the weakness and eccentricity which marked the movement. He gives graphic descriptions of the Syrian solitaries among whom he spent five years (374–9) in the desert of Chalcis. Here he found the tendency was to abandon the coenobitic life and to substitute the eremitic—a process the very opposite to what he afterwards found prevailing in Egypt. It was the home, too, of the "grazers," *i.e.* monks who at mealtimes went out into the fields and ate grass like cattle, and of the pillar saints like Simeon Stylites whose column was repeatedly lengthened till at last it was sixty feet in height. So great a power did he become that his advice was sought and taken as to whether or not the decrees of Chalcedon should be maintained. At first Jerome, like so many others, was completely carried away by the attractions of the eremite life, and in a rapturous outburst writes to Heliodorus who had withdrawn from it, as follows:—

"O desertum Christi floribus vernans, O solitudo in qua illi nascuntur lapides de quibus in Apocalypsi

42 THE EPISTLES OF ST. JEROME

civitas magni Regis exstruitur ! O eremus familiarius Deo gaudens " (xiv. 10).

But such rhapsodies were qualified not only by tears and groans caused by the haunting memories of his earlier life at Rome, but by the fierce controversies of his companions who, though living apart for most purposes, seemed to find many opportunities of association. Their bitter wrangling over the administrative and doctrinal questions which vexed the Church of Antioch, proved too much even for Jerome, who at last came to the conclusion that it was preferable to live among wild beasts than among such Christians ! (xvii. 8).

He has left, too, a fairly exhaustive account of Egyptian Monachism.* Arriving there in 386 he found three classes of monks.

(1) *The Remoboth or Sarabaitae.*—These Antonians, he says, had no settled rule, but lived together in groups of two and three, rarely in larger numbers, and generally in populous places. Jerome says they were unworthy of their profession, being cunning, quarrelsome, and greedy. They made a great parade of fasting and yet gorged to excess on feast days, and were not above suspicion in their relations with women.

(2) *Anchorites.*—They go, he says, from the monastery to the desert and live on bread and salt alone. He traces their spiritual descent through Paul the hermit and Antony to St. John the Baptist.

(3) *Coenobites or Sauses* (Pachomian).—With them, he says, the first principle was obedience to a superior. They were divided into bodies of ten and of an

* See xxii. 34–86.

hundred, each tenth man having authority over nine others, and the hundredth having ten of these " deans " under him. They lived apart in separate cells, and could only visit each other after the ninth hour, except the " deans " whose duty it was to comfort troubled brethren. After the ninth hour they met together for psalmody, scripture-reading, and prayer; these were followed by an exposition, amid profound silence, of the portion for the day, given by a monk called " the father." When the discourse was finished, the assembly broke up, and each band of ten went with its " father " to its own table, which each of the ten took it in turn to serve for a week at a time. The meal consisted of bread, pulse, and vegetables with salt for the only seasoning and with wine for the very old. Sick monks were carefully nursed by the old men in a spacious chamber. Lent was strictly observed, while Sundays were spent in prayer and reading.

The above quotations from his letter to Eustochium are given out of chronological sequence in order to complete his picture of Monachism in the East Jerome, however, on leaving the Syrian desert in 379 and before going to Egypt in 386, went first to Antioch, where he was ordained by Paulinus, then to Constantinople, and finally to Rome, where for three years (382–5) with unceasing zeal he devoted himself to the ascetic cause. He became the spiritual director of a band of aristocratic women, their guide, philosopher, and friend, their final and infallible court of appeal. To them he commended celibacy as the only perfect life—it was the hundredfold of the good seed of the Gospel, while widowhood was the sixty-fold, and wedlock the thirty-fold (cxxiii. 9, and xxii. 15). Practically, the only useful purpose served by marriage was that it produced virgins, as thorns produce a rose, or earth gold, or the shell a pearl (xxii. 20); mothers who devoted their daughters to the celibate life became " mothers-in-law of God " (xxii. 20). The success with which he preached these doctrines is everywhere evident in his epistles, and the revolution he wrought in the lives of these women may be gauged from his letter to Marcella in which he vividly contrasts Blesilla's past and present manner of life.

"In days gone by our widow was somewhat fastidious in her adornment and used to spend the whole day before her mirror to correct its deficiencies. Now she boldly says, 'We all with unveiled face, beholding as in a glass the glory of the Lord, are changed into the same image from glory to glory, even as by the Spirit of the Lord.' Then maids arranged her hair—the harmless top of which was held in its place by curled headbands. Now she leaves her head alone, and her only head-dress is a veil. Then a soft feather bed seemed hard to her . . . now she rises betimes for prayer . . . she kneels on the bare ground and with frequent tears cleanses a face once defiled with white lead " (xxxviii. 4).

Asella, dedicated before birth to virginity, consecrated when hardly more than ten years old (xxiv. 2), lived from her twelfth year by her own choice as follows:—

"Shut up in a narrow cell, she roamed through Paradise. Fasting was her recreation, hunger her refreshment. If she took food, it was not from love

THE ASCETIC AND MONASTIC MOVEMENT 45

of eating, but because of bodily exhaustion; and the bread and salt and cold water to which she restricted herself, sharpened her appetite more than they appeased it" (xxiv. 3).

So absorbed is Jerome in promoting the practice of asceticism that he writes to mothers telling them in minutest detail how to train their daughters from infancy as Church virgins; cvii. (ad Laetam) is perhaps his greatest effort in this direction, but xxii. addressed to Eustochium—then a girl of seventeen—is more remarkable still for the unreserved freedom and fullness with which it handles the sins and temptations of the flesh and the supposed consequent necessity of a celibate life. cxxx. is another illustration (a little milder and less fanatical in tone than xxii.) of the extreme lengths to which Jerome carried his ascetic teaching. Nothing can exceed the extravagance with which St. Jerome, who was an experienced man of the world, celebrates the self-devotion of Demetrias to the virgin state. Her family, like so many others of the great Roman houses, had been ruined by the invasion of Alaric. Rome had been given up to fire and sword. The fairest provinces were already overrun by the Sueves and Goths. The fame of a world-wide empire and civilisation, the splendid traditions and the hopes of senatorial houses of immemorial antiquity, were vanishing amid an agony of regret, all the more pathetic because hardly a voice from it comes down to our ears. Yet the devotion of Demetrias to the virgin state, according to her eulogist, exalts her family to a higher pinnacle than its long line of consuls and prefects have ever reached :

"*it is a consolation for Rome in ashes; Italy puts off its mourning* at the news; the villages in the farthest provinces are beside themselves with joy. Good Jesus! What exaltation there was all through the house! Many virgins sprouted at once as shoots from a fruitful stem, and the example set by their patroness and mistress was followed by a host of clients and servants. Virginity was warmly taken up in every house, and although those who professed it were of lower rank than Demetrias, yet they sought one reward with her, viz. that of chastity. My words are much too weak—every Church in Africa danced from very joy. The news reached not only the cities, towns, and villages, but even the scattered huts. Every island between Africa and Italy was full of it.... You would fancy the Goths had been annihilated" (cxxx. 6).

But the climax of this highly rhetorical passage is reached when the writer goes on to declare that

"there was less elation in Rome when Marcellus defeated Hannibal at Nola, than when the news came that Demetrias had taken the vow of virginity—though thousands of Romans had fallen at the Trebia, Thrasymenus, and Cannae. There was less joy among the nobles cooped up in the capitol on whom the future of Rome depended, when, after buying their lives with gold, they heard that the Gauls had at length been routed" (cxxx. 6).

It is easier to credit Jerome when in the same passage he states that there were mothers with little faith who dedicated only their deformed, crippled, and unmarriageable daughters. Still, exaggerated and perfervid as the whole letter is, it witnesses to the hold which the movement had taken at any rate upon

THE ASCETIC AND MONASTIC MOVEMENT 47

some of the Christian community and serves to illustrate the statement made in cxxvii. 8, that Rome had become a " second Jerusalem."

Not only women, however, yielded to the spell of the ascetic spirit. Men, too, were won over. There was, *e.g.*, Bonosus who lived a hermit life on an island in the Adriatic (vii. 3). There were the wealthy and well-born Florentius, Pammachius a senator and patrician, Toxotius, and many others. Neither the edicts of emperors, nor the protests of parents were able to suppress or even check it. Jerome was the oracle whose words were the supreme law, and his consistent teaching was that eating and drinking, marriage and even personal ablutions were low physical indulgences to be disparaged and discouraged, when they could not be altogether discarded. Virginity was the ideal, if not the essential Christian life. The soul like Abraham must go out from its own land and kindred, and to it must be applied the words of the Psalmist (xlv. ii. 12): "Hearken, O daughter, and consider, incline thine ear: forget also thine own people and thy father's house. So shall the King have pleasure in thy beauty" (Letter xxii. 1).

How to account for this enthusiasm of asceticism, what it was which induced Fabiola to build the first Christian hospital, and the wealthy Paula to renounce friends and fortune and to die in debt—are questions not easy to adequately answer.

(1) Jerome's impassioned pleading was, no doubt, a chief cause, but not even his compelling eloquence could have met with the success it did, if the soil had not been in some degree prepared.

(2) Dean Fremantle, in his prolegomena to

Jerome's letters (p. xxxi.) remarks truly enough that
" certain states of the human mind seem all-pervasive
like the causes of diseases which spring up at once
in many different places." The spirit was working
in other parts of the world as well as Rome. Buddha
was a name familiar to Jerome; so also were the
Brahmans and Gymnosophists of India, to the former
of whom Demetrius of Alexandria sent Pantaenus as
a missionary (lxx. 4). Asceticism, therefore, was in
the air, and its presence at Rome was scarcely a
matter for surprise.

(3) But it was the social and political condition
of the world which helped to water the ground. The
empire was tottering, and the outlook to patriotic
souls was dark indeed.

" The grace which is completely absent from the
great Christian writers of that epoch (fourth and fifth
centuries) is hope. Such hope as is found even in the
Civitas Dei of Augustine is entirely that of the world
to come. The world before them seemed hopelessly
corrupt " (Fremantle xxxi.).

The ascetic movement appealed strongly to what
remained among Romans of pristine simplicity and
sternness, and was welcomed as a reaction from the
luxury and effeminacy of the day. If anything could
save the State from ruin and decay, it was a return
to the hardihood of earlier times. The favourable
reception given to the doctrines of Jerome, was a sign
that the old Roman spirit, however generally moribund, was not altogether extinct. But while some
supported him for this reason, others saw in the movement a very different tendency. As Sir S. Dill puts
it, on p. 12 of his book :

THE ASCETIC AND MONASTIC MOVEMENT 49

"Such a movement might well seem to an old-fashioned Roman a renunciation not only of citizenship, but of all the hard-won fruits of civilisation, and social life.

"If this was the highest form of Christian life, as its devotees proclaimed it to be, then Christianity was the foe, not only of the old religion, but of the social and political order which Rome had given to the world. It is hardly to be wondered at that the monks were execrated alike by the mob and by the cultivated pagan noble."

It may have been some such fear, and not merely resentment at the extreme austerity she had been taught to practise, which made the mob cry at Blesilla's funeral: "Quousque genus detestabile non urbe pellitur ? non lapidibus obruitur ?" (xxxix. 5).

(4) The *moral corruption* of Roman society as evidenced in the pages both of Jerome and Marcellinus, would drive the best men, in sheer disgust, to the opposite extreme. How deep the corruption was, the former plainly shows. Speaking from first-hand knowledge he says in cxvii. 6 of Roman banquets: "Difficile inter epulas servatur pudicitia." It is a terrible picture of Roman women in cxxvii. 3 :

"while they mourn for their husbands they have lost, they rejoice at their own deliverance and at their freedom to choose fresh partners—not, as God wills, to obey them, but to rule over them. With this end in view they select for their partners poor men who, contented with the mere name of husband, are the more ready to put up with rivals, as they know that if they so much as murmur they will be cast off at once."

Worse still is what he says in cxxviii. 3 :

"I am ashamed to say it, yet I must; ladies of

noble birth who have rejected more high-born suitors, cohabit with men who are of the lowest grade, and even with slaves. Sometimes in the name of religion and under pretence of desire for celibacy they actually desert their husbands in favour of such paramours. One may often see a Helen following her Paris without the smallest dread of Menelaus. Such persons we see and mourn for, but we cannot punish them, for the multitude of sinners secures tolerance for the sin."

It is hardly to be wondered at under such conditions, that Jerome, like some Old Testament prophet, should insist that the only effectual protest and the only sure salvation lay in complete separation and withdrawal from the world, nor is it a matter for surprise that he should regard the fall of Rome as the consequence and just punishment of its corruption; and that, when the news of it reached him, he should heap together Bible passages on the destruction of Jerusalem and Virgil's lines on the sack of Troy. It was to him the sure and certain judgment of Heaven on its flagrant vices, and it brought to the saint and his disciples the final and crowning proof of their conviction that the celibate, ascetic, monastic life was the only safe course for those who would stand in the evil day.

(5) *There was the corruption of the Church.*—Christianity had lost its first fervour. With the cessation of martyrdoms and persecutions, trouble was transferred from without to within. A reaction begins, and earlier in this volume an attempt has been made to show how the clergy of the towns became infected with worldliness and even with worse vices,

THE ASCETIC AND MONASTIC MOVEMENT 51

and how, after allowing for Jerome's tendency to monkish exaggeration, the conclusion is compelled that he is describing the rule and not the exception. Naturally, under such circumstances, it seemed impossible to the faithful remnant to live the Christian life in the Sybarite society of the second Babylon, when unworthy pastors betrayed their trust, and when the rank and file of the Church consisted largely of nominal adherents who had come over to the new religion from lowest motives—favour with the ruling powers, fashion, social advancement, and such like.

The above are some of the chief reasons which underlay a most remarkable chapter of ecclesiastical history, a chapter which does not close for nearly a thousand years after the death of its great protagonist, a chapter, too, which is almost inevitable at a time of imperial decay and degenerate Christianity. It is impossible to be blind to the moral grandeur of the ascetic movement as illustrated, *e.g.*, in the life of Paula or Eustochium, with its immense sacrifice, its endurance to the end, its complete submission to what it conceived to be the call and will of God, its renunciation of former luxury and comfort, its wholehearted devotion to poverty and prayer, for the Kingdom of Heaven's sake. Probably the world since Jerome's day has seen few such perfect acts of self-denial as those which this Latin Father fostered and inspired. Even Gibbon speaks with appreciation of them, though he cannot refrain from a characteristic sneer:

" In the capital of the Empire, females of noble and opulent houses possessed a very ample share of independent property, and many of these devout

52 THE EPISTLES OF ST. JEROME

females had embraced the doctrines of Christianity not only with the cold assent of the understanding but with the warmth of affection, and perhaps with the eagerness of fashion " (" Decline and Fall of the Roman Empire," chap. xxv. p. 253).

But at the same time, sympathy is due to Vigilantius and the other critics of Jerome in their protests against his exaggerated view of virginity as the one and only perfect way of life, and his equally unreasonable depreciation of God's ordinance of matrimony—*e.g.* when in cxvii. 3 he describes it as a plank for a shipwrecked man (" Secunda post naufragium tabula est, quod male coeperis saltem hoc remedio, temperare "). Well, indeed, may Dr. T. R. Glover remark in his " Life and Letters in the Fourth Century," p. 127 : " Jerome is never so copious or so coloured as when he dilates on the glory of celibacy, and the poverty, pettiness, and ignominy of married life." He failed to recognise that the asceticism he preached was at variance with human nature itself. He forgot or ignored the fact that men must render to Cæsar as well as to God. He could not see that Christianity would never conquer the world by withdrawal from it, or that its Founder intended it to leaven the whole lump of human society—a task it could not achieve in isolation or aloofness from it. If the Church is to do the work its Head has charged it to do, it must not hide itself in the dens and caves of the earth, but come out into the open and let its light shine before men. If Jerome had pleaded that the times were exceptionally evil and needed an exceptional remedy, if he had been anxious to prove to the pagan world the strength of the Christian

THE ASCETIC AND MONASTIC MOVEMENT 53

religion—a strength so great that it enabled a man to make the greatest acts of renunciation, he would have been on unassailable ground. His mistake was to regard asceticism, especially in the form of monasticism, as an end in itself. He does not seem to have ever thoroughly considered its philosophy or to have troubled about its inner spirit. For this we have to turn to Cassian's "Collations," where in the very foreground of his work he gives an exposition of its theory and purpose, the Abbot Moses declaring its true aim to be the attainment of purity of heart,

" so that the mind may rest fixed on God and divine things ; for this purpose only are fastings, watchings, meditation of Scripture, solitude, privations to be undertaken ; such asceticisms are not perfection, but only the instruments of perfection." ("Cambridge Mediaeval History," vol. i. p. 525.)

To view, however, asceticism and extreme asceticism, as Jerome did, as an end in itself, as a rule for all and sundry, always and everywhere, was to set up an impossible standard. It was to impress on men the ideals of St. John the Baptist rather than those of Christ, who blessed the wedding feast of Cana with His presence and first miracle that He wrought, Who ate and drank with publicans and sinners, and gave us all things richly to enjoy.

THE COMMUNION OF ST. JEROME

A REMINISCENCE OF THE VATICAN GALLERY

See Jerome sinking at the goal of life,
The toil for ever done, and hush'd the strife !
The war of soul with sense, the war of thought,
Long, loud and keen, with saint and sinner fought,
The studious labours o'er the heaven-given page,
Text, version, comment, plied from youth to age,
While the stern scholar, working on unspent,
Pil'd for all time his letter'd monument—
All, all is over now ; and what remains ?
What prop the once so fiery heart sustains ?
No pride of cultur'd reason moves him here,
No sense of hard-won knowledge, vast and clear ;
The faded eyes, with upward glances meek,
His Lord, in Sacrament presented, seek ;
Christ is his all, for pardon, life and rest,
And the man dies, believing, on His breast.

BISHOP HANDLEY MOULE.

IV

ROME AND THE ROMAN SEE

IN his "History of Latin Christianity" (vol. i. chap. ii. p. 86) Dean Milman says—

"The great offices which still perpetuated in name the ancient Republic, the Senatorship, Quaestorship, Consulate, are quietly transmitted according to the Imperial mandates, excite no popular commotion, nor even interest, for they are honorary titles which confer neither influence, authority, nor wealth. Even the prefecture of the city is accepted at the will of the Emperor who rarely condescends to visit Rome. But the election to the Bishopric is now not merely an affair of importance, *the* affair of paramount importance, it might seem in Rome—it is an event in the annals of the world."

This statement is scarcely an exaggeration. It is confirmed by the story which Jerome tells of the pagan prefect of the city—Vettius Praetextatus—that he was wont to say to Pope Damasus, "Make me Bishop of Rome and I will at once become a Christian" (ad Pammachium, Adv. John of Jerusalem, section 8). It is further supported by the heathen historian Ammianus Marcellinus, who, in Book XXVII.

56   THE EPISTLES OF ST. JEROME

chap. iii. sections 12, 13, 14, describes the bitter conflict for the papacy between Damasus and Ursinus in A.D. 366, a conflict which proves that it was now a greatly coveted prize—

" Damasus et Ursinus supra humanum modum ad rapiendam episcopatus sedem ardentes, scissis studiis asperrime conflictabantur, ad usque mortis vulnerumque discrimina adjumentis utriusque progressis. . . ."

So fierce was the strife that on one day one hundred and thirty-seven dead bodies were found—and then Marcellinus adds that the combatants were not quarrelling about nothing, since the successful candidate had no further cause for fear in the future, for the Bishops of Rome grew wealthy by the offerings of matrons, rode in grand carriages when they went out, wore dignified robes, and gave such lavish banquets that they surpassed even royal entertainments. Evidently in the latter half of the fourth century the Papacy had reached a pitch of dignity and influence sufficient to impress itself strongly on the imagination of contemporary cultured pagans.

A variety of causes had contributed to place the See and Church of Rome in this exalted position, a position to which Ignatius testifies as early as A.D. 112 when, in his epistle to the Romans, he expresses his fear that their weighty influence will be exerted to deprive him of the honour of martyrdom. Among these causes may be mentioned—

(1) *The reputed Apostolic foundation of the Church and See.*—It was the only Church in Christendom, with the exception of Antioch, which claimed to have

two Apostles as its founders, and those two the very chief of "the glorious company." It was the only Apostolic See in the West. For this claim there is the support, from the second century onwards, of a strong and persistent local tradition. Irenaeus is the first to mention the double apostolic foundation, but Jerome, in his "De Viris Illustribus," section I., supplies the fullest details, so far at any rate as St. Peter is concerned. "Simon Peter, the prince of the Apostles, in the second year of the Emperor Claudius . . . came to Rome, and there for twenty-five years occupied the episcopal throne till the last year of Nero." As the desire grew to apply the Petrine texts of the New Testament to the Bishops of Rome, less and less is heard in this connection of St. Paul and more and more of St. Peter. It was (as Mr. Turner remarks in the "Cambridge Mediæval History," vol. i. pp. 172–3) from the pontificate of Damasus that there

" dates the first definite self-expression of the Papacy, when much that had been fluid, immature, tentative was crystallised into a hard and fast system. It fell to the able and masterful Damasus in the last years of a long life and troubled pontificate, to attempt what his predecessors had not yet attempted and to formulate, in brief and incisive terms, the doctrine of Rome upon creed and Bible and Pope. . . ." A " Council in 382 published the first official Canon of Scripture in the West—the influence of Jerome, at that time papal secretary, is traceable in it—and the first official definition of papal claims. Roman primacy ('ceteris ecclesiis praelata,' 'primatum obtinuit') is grounded . . . directly on the promise of Christ to Peter."

58 THE EPISTLES OF ST. JEROME

It is probably the mind of Damasus which is reflected in the utterances of Jerome. In letters xv. and xvi. he professes himself the very humble and dutiful servant of the See of Rome. Its Bishop he regards as the successor of the Fisherman.* Its soil brings forth an hundredfold. He that gathers not with it scattereth. To Damasus he appeals to decide (i) which of three claimants to the See of Antioch was its rightful bishop; (ii) whether it is correct to speak of three hypostases in the Godhead or of one, for, he says, " he who clings to the See of Peter is accepted by me " (xvi. 2). This is the Rock on which the Church is built. This is the house where alone the Pascal Lamb is rightly eaten. This is the Ark of Noah and whosoever is not found in it perishes when the flood prevails (xv. 2). This alleged apostolic foundation was a priceless asset to the papacy, and astute Pontiffs were quick to turn it to practical account, making the Roman bishopric more and more a Court of Appeal. Thus, replying to certain questions which Himerius of Tarragona had addressed to Damasus, Siricius rests his authority on his duty, as successor of St. Peter, to " bear the burden of all who are heavily laden," or rather on the ground that "the blessed Apostle Peter bears them in us, for he, as we trust, in all things protects and defends us who are the heirs of his government." Here Siricius strikes the note which was sounded more loudly and clearly some seventy years later by Leo I., who exercised an authority over the Catholic Church as a whole, vaguer, indeed, but

* *Cf.* Adv. Luciferians 23, where Stephen is called " the blessed Peter's twenty-second successor in the See of Rome."

ROME AND THE ROMAN SEE

not less real than that of a bishop in his diocese.—Kidd. iii. 390.

(2) *The Character of its Bishops* was also no small factor in its greatness. A few, like Damasus, Innocent, Leo, were men of strong personality who left an impress on the Roman bishopric only a little less pronounced than that of Cyprian on the See of Carthage or that of Ambrose on Milan. But, for the most part, the Bishops of Rome were chosen not for showy or brilliant gifts, or for personal or official distinction in other walks of life. They were, as a rule, clerics who had risen through the usual " cursus honorum," men well versed in affairs and of considerable experience of the practical work of the Church; not given to theological speculation, but good administrators and disciplinarians, of orthodox views, who earned the confidence of the Church generally, contributing not a little by their solid qualities to the stability of the Roman See and to its influence throughout Christendom.

(3) *Its Orthodoxy.*—Though not a great theological centre, like Alexandria, yet the Church of Rome was endowed with a splendid capacity for holding the tradition. In spite of occasional failures, like Liberius and Honorius, the orthodoxy of the Popes was conspicuous through all the controversies on the Trinity and the Incarnation. It was a great tribute to the soundness of its doctrine when the East accepted the Tome of Damasus with its sober Catholic theology, just as some seventy years later it accepted the Tome of Leo. As far back as 112 A.D. Ignatius in his epistle to the Romans had declared the Church " free from every foreign dye."

60 THE EPISTLES OF ST. JEROME

(4) *Its Organisation.*—Besides the bishop there were in Rome in the time of Pope Cornelius, 46 presbyters, 7 deacons, 7 sub-deacons, 42 acolytes, exorcists and ushers, and over 1,500 widows and poor; each deacon had charge of one of the seven ecclesiastical regions into which Fabian had divided the city. It was probably an allusion to its excellent organisation when Decius declared he would rather hear of a rival emperor than of a bishop set up in Rome.

(5) *Its Charity.*—Ignatius in A.D. 112, in the opening paragraph of his epistle to the Romans, speaks of the Church of Rome as "holding the chief place in love." As it had supremacy of rank among the Churches round about it, so, too, was it foremost among them in works of charity. Possibly in this passage, Ignatius is assigning to the Roman Church a position of priority among the Churches of the *world* both in rank and in love. Dionysius of Corinth (A.D. 175) testifies to the world-wide charity of the Roman Church (Euseb. H.E. iv. 23).

(6) *Need of a Centre.*—Jerome, writing to Rusticus, enforces by various analogies the expediency of admitting a central and single authority. He adduces examples from the animal kingdom, the imperial power, judicial and military power, and from domestic life, and finally goes on to say "singuli ecclesiarum episcopi, singuli archipresbyteri, singuli archidiaconi, et omnis ordo ecclesiasticis suis rectoribus nititur" (cxxv.), yet oddly enough makes no reference to the Bishop of Rome in this connection. Still the need for a strong central authority in matters of faith and discipline was growing greater almost daily and finds expression

ROME AND THE ROMAN SEE 61

in the Canon of Sardica allowing deposed bishops to refer their case to Rome. Events in the secular world were moving in the same direction. The decay of the Western Empire, the removal of the seat of government from Rome, left the old traditions of authority and the prestige of the eternal city to add lustre to the papal throne, whose possessors became more and more important as paganism died out and as each new Western Emperor was feebler than the last. The influx of barbarian invaders also demanded, in the interests of society no less than of religion, a strong centre of moral and social authority. Ecclesiastical Rome stood ready to hand for this purpose, and, as there was no adequate rival, was soon the unquestioned arbiter and oracle to nations hardly less than to Churches.

(7) *Secular Prominence.*—Though some Church historians dispute it, there can be little doubt that the civil status of the capital contributed considerably to the ecclesiastical greatness of Rome. Rome was known as the mistress of the world, and it was the inevitable consequence that the Roman Church should be regarded, consciously or unconsciously, as the mother and mistress of other Churches. Had apostolic foundation been the only factor in determining the importance of a Church, Antioch—founded by SS. Peter and Paul—would have taken precedence of Alexandria—whose founder was St. Mark—whereas Alexandria was reckoned the second city of the empire and Antioch the third; almost certainly, therefore, it may be concluded that the secular status and dignity of the capital served to enhance the glory of the Church of Rome.

(8) *Rescripts of Valentinian and Gratian.*—These conferred on the Pope a large measure of jurisdiction over the whole Western Empire, giving a certain legal sanction to his official acts, and among these acts to the letters which he sent out, from time to time, in response to the requests for advice which came to him from the provinces.

Jerome in his letters accepts the Roman supremacy and, as shown above, treats the bishop with an almost servile deference. In lxxxiv. 8 he entreats the Origenists to spare the faith of a Church which an Apostle has praised. In lxiii. 2 he reminds Theophilus that his (Jerome's) aim is always to remember the faith of Rome.

In cxxvii. 9 he speaks of the " clear waters of the faith of Rome;" while in cxxxvii. Pope Innocent severely censures John of Jerusalem for his supine handling of the Pelagian riots at Bethlehem. But in cxlvi. 2 Jerome completely changes his attitude to the See of Rome :

" You will say how comes it that at Rome a priest is only ordained on the recommendation of a deacon ? Why do you mention a custom which only prevails in one city ? Why do you oppose to the general law of the Church a *paltry exception* which has given rise to arrogance and pride ? " "If you ask for authority, the world outweighs its capital."

Such language strikes a very different note from his former utterances. Now he insists on the essential equality of all bishops,

" whether it be at Rome or Gubbio, at Constantinople or at Rhegium, at Alexandria or at Zoan, a bishop's

ROME AND THE ROMAN SEE 63

dignity and priesthood are one. Neither the command of wealth nor the lowliness of poverty make him more a bishop, or less a bishop. All alike are successors of the Apostles."

Possibly closer acquaintance with the clergy of the capital, whom he so mercilessly satirises, had weakened his previous admiration for everything papal. Possibly his changed view may be attributed to his disappointment at his non-election to Rome's chief dignity on the death of Damasus. In xlv. 3 he remarks, pathetically, "omnium paene judicio dignus summo sacerdotio decernebar." However explained, the altered attitude of Jerome is striking and remarkable.

But of temporal Rome he remained to the last a devoted son. Its capture by Alaric seemed to him the end of all things—he " forgot his own name " (cxxvi. 2); " the world sinks into ruin because the famous city is swallowed up in one tremendous fire " (cxxviii. 4); he can only quote the psalmist, " O God, the heathen are come into Thine inheritance " (cxxvii. 2); " The bright light of all the world was put out, the whole world perished in one city " (Preface to Ezekiel). He could not foresee that the humiliation of *Imperial* Rome meant the increased importance of the Papacy.

"Honorius hid himself in Ravenna, nor did the Emperor ever again for any long time make his residence at Rome. . . . The capture of Rome by Alaric was one of the great steps by which the Pope rose to his plenitude of power. There could be no question that from this time the greatest man in Rome was the Pope."—Milman, " History of Latin Christianity," Book II. i. 139.

V

PROGRESS OF THE CHURCH

VERY little is known as to the progress of the Church in the early centuries. The duty of extending its frontiers was, however, clearly recognised, for prayers for the conversion of the heathen are found both in the Eastern and Western liturgies. No definite organisation seems to have existed for purposes of propaganda, and it was left entirely to the initiative of individual bishops and priests to carry out or neglect the last command of Christ. Justin Martyr (Dial. C. 117) and Tertullian (Apol. 37; Adv. Judaeos 7) speak of Asia Minor, Greece, Italy, South Gaul, and North Africa as having, in or before their time, submitted to the Christian faith, though they give no details as to the missionary methods employed. At a later date the information becomes more precise and complete. Ulphilas, *e.g.*, " the apostle of the Goths," in 325 devotes himself exclusively to the conversion of his countrymen and of a considerable colony of farm labourers which he had formed on the slopes of Mt. Haemus.

" Equally efficient as a missionary and organiser " he " gathered and united the scattered confessors of the Christian Faith, and by his enthusiastic preaching of the Gospel won for it many adherents . . . not

PROGRESS OF THE CHURCH 65

least so in virtue of his great work of translating the Bible by which he transmitted to his people the knowledge of the Holy Scriptures for all time."— " Cambridge Mediæval History," p. 212.

Eusebius, Bishop of Vercelli, 340–371, made his cathedral a centre of missionary operations, while Chrysostom in 404 founded a college at Constantinople in which Goths were to be trained for propaganda work among their own people. Indeed, so devoted was Chrysostom to the cause that even in exile he still supported it by writing letters and collecting funds. A little later the foundation of Honoratus in the island of Lerins became a stronghold of missionary labour. It gave bishops to Arles, Troyes, Avignon, Lyons, Metz, and Nice, who not only faithfully discharged their diocesan duties to their own flocks, but attacked, vigorously, the surrounding heathenism. The work of extension was greatly facilitated by the excellent Roman roads, the decline of the old piracy, the peace which, generally speaking, prevailed throughout the Empire in spite of frontier fighting, and the widespread habit of travel in the fourth and fifth centuries.

It was in the West where aggressive pioneer work was most actively carried on, though, even so, the Western Church was far behind the Eastern in the first five centuries, the latter having had, of course, a hundred years' start of the former. In 312 half the population of the East was Christian, but only one-tenth of that of the West. In the East the monks of the Thebaid did indeed penetrate as far as Phœnicia and beyond the Euphrates, sowing the Gospel seed, but sowing it apparently very superficially, for even before the armies of Mahomet swept away the Christian communities they founded, inaction and lethargy set in and evangelistic work considerably declined, if it did not altogether die out. Perhaps the very close association between Church and State in the East did not conduce to vigorous spiritual life. Ecclesiastical divisions were practically coterminous with the civil, the emperor was regarded with excessive veneration and Constantine was ἰσαπόστολος. There was no such feeling in the West, where Rome was everything and where Jerome could say, at its fall in 410, that the human race was involved in its ruin.

Jerome was born some twenty years after the outward triumph of orthodox Christianity at the Council of Nicaea, when the then defeated Arianism was again raising its head and was about to actually seat itself on the throne of the Cæsars in the person of Constantius (351–61). He would be still a schoolboy when the pagan reaction took place under Julian (361–63). He would be in the prime of life when Arianism received its mortal wounds (1) at Adrianople in the defeat and death of Valens in 378, and (2) at the Council of Constantinople in 381, after which it became more and more a religion of barbarians. Yet though he had seen all this ebb and flow, his language in the epistles, and elsewhere, bears emphatic and consistent witness to the progress of the Church, a witness which is far too favourable and is unconfirmed or even contradicted by other authorities. Writing in 386 (xlvi. 2, Migne) Paula says :

" Rome has a holy Church, trophies of Apostles and Martyrs, a true confession of Christ. The faith

PROGRESS OF THE CHURCH 67

has been preached there by an Apostle, *heathenism has been trodden down, the name of Christ is daily exalted higher and higher.*"

Again in 396, writing to Heliodorus (lx. 4) he says :

" Now the voices and writings of *all nations* proclaim the Passion and Resurrection of Christ. I say nothing of the Jews, the Greeks, and the Romans, peoples which the Lord has dedicated to His faith by the title written on His Cross. The immortality of the soul and its continuance after the dissolution of the body, truths of which Pythagoras dreamed, which Democritus refused to believe, which Socrates debated in prison . . . are now the familiar themes of Indian and Persian, of Goth and of Egyptian. The fierce Bessians and the throng of skin-clad savages who used to offer human sacrifices in honour of the dead, have broken out of their harsh discord into the sweet music of the Cross, and *Christ is the one cry of the whole world.*"

Similarly in lxvi. 4, writing to a Roman Senator named Pammachius in 397, he declares, " In our time Rome possesses that of which the world was ignorant in the past. Then few of the wise, mighty, and noble were Christians, now many wise, powerful, and noble are even monks."

In the treatise against Helvidius, section 4, he writes : " Now that the *whole world* has embraced the faith," etc.

Again, writing to Laeta in 403 (cvii. 1, 2) he says :

" For all its gilding the Capitol looks dingy ; every temple in Rome is covered with soot and cobwebs. The city is stirred to its foundations, and the people rush past their half-ruined shrines to go to the tombs of the martyrs. . . . Did not your own Gracchus—whose name signifies patrician birth—when a few years ago he held the prefecture of the city, overthrow, smash and shake to pieces the grotto of Mithras * and all the dreadful images within it ? those, I mean, by which the devotee is initiated as Raven, Bridegroom, Soldier, Lion, Perseus, Sun, Crab, Father ? Did he not, I say, destroy these, and then, sending them before him as hostages, obtain for himself Christian baptism ? Even in Rome itself paganism is left in solitude. They who once were the gods of the nations remain under their lonely roofs with horned owls and birds of night. The standards of the military are emblazoned with the sign of the Cross. The Emperor's robes of purple and his diadem sparkling with jewels are adorned with representations of the shameful yet saving gibbet. Already the Egyptian Serapis † has been made a Christian; while at Gaza Marnas ‡ mourns in con-

* The Persian sun-god. Mithraism was the greatest of all the Mystery religions both in influence and extension. Flourishing 50 years B.C. it reached world-wide importance in the second century A.D. At its core lay the ancient Persian Dualism which regarded life as a struggle between good and evil. Then it passed under Babylonian influence and acquired some degree of nature-worship and a strong element of astrology. Mithras is a mediator between the supreme god and mankind, and his blood saves humanity. There are some decided resemblances between it and Christianity—*e.g.* Mithraism had baptism, confirmation, and a Eucharist and pure ascetic ethics. It observed Sunday, and the 25th of December was the birthday of Mithras. But it differed from Christianity in (1) being a military religion—its monuments, altars, etc., being found chiefly on the military frontiers where life was hardest; (2) it gave no position in the cult to women. It was a formidable rival to the Church and was not overthrown till the fourth century. The names Corax, Nymphus, Miles, etc., were the symbols of stars and planets; Mithraics taking one or other of the names at their initiation.

† Temple of Serapis at Alexandria was destroyed in 389 and a Christian church built upon its site.

‡ An idol god of Gaza—mentioned also in Jerome's "Life of Hilarion," section 20.

PROGRESS OF THE CHURCH 69

finement and expects every moment to see his temple overturned. From India, from Persia, from Ethiopia, we daily welcome monks in crowds. The Armenian bowman has laid aside his quiver, the Huns learn the psalter, the chilly Scythians are warmed with the glow of the faith. The Getae, ruddy and yellow-haired, carry tent-churches about with their armies: and perhaps their success in fighting against us may be due to the fact that they believe in the same religion."

Another striking testimony to the advance of Christianity occurs in Jerome's Preface to his commentary on the Galatians.

"How few there are who now read Aristotle! How many are there who know the books or even the name of Plato? You may find, here and there, a few old men who have nothing else to do, who study them in a corner. But the *whole world* speaks the language of our Christian peasants and fishermen, the *whole world* re-echoes their words."

Jerome's repeated assertions that the world was now Christian must be dismissed as a gross exaggeration. Dr. Maclear, in the "Dictionary of Christian Antiquities" (article "Missions") says that

"the close of the eighth century did not see even the half of Europe won over, even in the most nominal form, to the Cross of Christ. The whole of the great Scandinavian peninsula, all Bulgaria, Bohemia, Moravia, Russia, Poland, Pomerania, Prussia, and Lithuania remained to be evangelised. In most countries no missionary had ever set foot, or if he had, was obliged to retire at once before the furious opposition of heathen tribes. Even at the close of the fourth century, after Christianity had enjoyed, during more than sixty years, the sunshine of imperial favour, the Christians at Antioch, a city which had well-nigh greater spiritual advantages than any other, constituted only about half of the population (Chrys. Op. Tom. ii. 567; vii. 810), and more than fifty years after the conversion of Constantine, the cultivated and influential classes of old Latin Rome still remained heathen, while the word 'peasant' synonymous with 'unbeliever' tells its own tale. In the fifth century Leo, Bishop of Rome, deplores the deep corruption even of Christian society and adjures his flock not to fall back into heathenism."

The Eleusinian and other mysteries continued to attract crowds of strangers till the Goths, under Alaric, destroyed its famous temple. Olympic games were celebrated till 394. The Prefect of Constantinople was a pagan in 404, and in 467 the quaestor of Antioch was accused of heathenism. Evidently Jerome had considerably underrated the tenacity of heathenism, even after its external suppression. He had not realised, in any adequate measure, the inherent conservatism of all religions—a conservatism which is especially obstinate when the religion is associated with patriotic reverence for a venerable past. Gratian might refuse the office of Pontifex Maximus and order that the cost of pagan sacrifices and ceremonies should no longer be charged to the imperial exchequer, but such summary action did not mean that heathenism was dead. The emphatic protest of the Senate, when he removed the Altar of Victory, witnesses to the contrary, as do also the outbreak of pagan feeling on the approach of Radagaisus and Alaric, and its temporary triumph under Attalus. He had scarcely grasped the fact that the new paganism of his day

PROGRESS OF THE CHURCH 71

was an infinitely higher and purer thing than the old. It was no longer the gods of Olympus satirised by the early apologists who confronted Christianity, but a religion which, in many of its distinctive doctrines, bore a strong resemblance to those taught by the Catholic Church. Even though Julian failed to make it an official substitute for the Christian Faith, it continued to be considerably practised in private, especially in the West. The Senate was strongly pagan and its members were proud to put on their tombstones that they had been priests of Isis or Mithras, while inscriptions and other archæological remains, not only at Rome but in the most distant provinces, prove the extent and vitality of this latter cult. The study of rhetoric, based as it was on the old mythology and on a belief in the eternal destiny of Rome, was another cause of the persistence of paganism. So, too, was the Neoplatonist philosophy which had a marked influence on the Greek and Syrian fathers—*e.g.* Basil and the two Gregories—and greatly affected Hilary and Augustine in the West. But the new heathenism did not appeal to the " common man." The world, too, had outgrown the magic and superstition with which it was still associated. Christianity had not only a compact organisation, but it was at once simpler and more profound. It had also an assimilating power which enabled it to gather up and absorb into itself all that was best in Roman civil life, and in rival religious systems.

Thus, while Jerome's repeated assertions that " the whole world " was Christian cannot, in their literality, be accepted, it is true, as Dr. Maclear declares :

"Slow . . . as was the actual rate of progress, there never was a period during these centuries (first to eighth) when the flood was not really rising, though the unobservant eye might not detect it . . . in the darkest times there were ever some streaks of light, and the leaven destined to quicken the mass of society was never wholly inert or ineffectual."—"Dictionary of Christian Antiquities," vol. ii. p. 1213.

VI

HERESIES AND SCHISMS

THE epistles of St. Jerome are of no little interest if only for the picture they present of the various schisms and heresies which troubled the Church of his day. It is evident from them that the Christian society in the fourth and fifth centuries was in a condition of anything but unruffled unity, especially in the East and to a minor degree in the West. Not only were there, *e.g.*, three claimants to the important See of Antioch, and rival bishops even of Rome, but there were, according to Epiphanius's letter to Jerome (li. 4), no less than eighty different heresies in existence, all " wresting the Scriptures to their own destruction." And if there was scarcely a limit to the *number* of the sects, still less was there a term to the strangeness and wild extravagance of their tenets. Jerome was clearly well acquainted with their doctrines, and very anxious to safeguard his disciples from falling into their errors, and perhaps, also, to build up for himself a reputation for orthodoxy of belief. At any rate his writings show how extensively these errors had been propagated and how deeply rooted still were some of the false teachings which had first seen the light long before his time.

(a) MONTANISM

The first of these movements with which he came into contact was Montanism. Dating from the middle of the second century, it was a reaction from, and a protest against, the still earlier Gnostic heresy. Gnosticism, in theory at any rate, had preached the supremacy of the intellect in the Christian life and the superiority of enlightenment to faith and conduct. Spiritual excellence consisted not in a holy life, but in γνῶσις of an esoteric kind open only to the initiated. Truth was thus represented as difficult of attainment and as the exclusive possession of a privileged few. Ordinary people might accept the Gospel in its literal and superficial sense, but there was a higher and deeper interpretation which only Gnostics could understand.

Against this excessive exaltation of knowledge, Montanism asserted the claims of emotion and even of ecstasy to a paramount place in the life of the spirit, much as in modern times the Methodist movement superseded and supplemented the latitudinarian. It demanded a place for the man in the street as well as for the man in the study. It was an inevitable reaction from an ultra-academic type of religion, insisting, as it did originally, on the need of simplicity and on our Lord's principle : " To the poor the Gospel is preached."

Its founder was Montanus, a native of Mysia, a convert to Christianity—who had probably been a priest of Cybele—for Jerome speaks of him in xli. 4 as " abscisum et semivirum." About A.D. 157 he gave himself out to be a prophet, maintaining that the office had not come to an end in the New Testament.

HERESIES AND SCHISMS

He spoke in frenzied speech which his enemies interpreted to mean demoniac possession, but which his friends declared to be the inspiration of God. He himself maintained that he was but a passive instrument in the hand of Heaven repeating the words which were put into his mouth; it was a case, he said, simply of the plectrum and the lyre, though his opponents insisted it was a blasphemous identification of himself with the Father.

Two women, Prisca in 175 and Maximilla in 179, left their husbands to join him, and contributed not a little to the later extravagances of the movement, urging that it was now the era of the Spirit and that the Second Advent was at hand. Of this final revelation Montanus, Prisca, and Maximilla declared themselves the only exponents, and, relying on apocalyptic and chiliastic passages in the Bible, settled at Pepuza in Phrygia, which they called the "New Jerusalem," to await the consummation of all things. Soon the Church began to get uneasy about their ecstatic utterances and two prelates tried to exorcise Prisca and Maximilla. Then the hierarchy of Asia Minor condemned their teaching by synodical action, and Rome, through the representations of Irenaeus and of Praxeas, also declined to countenance them. Montanism then came under the influence of smaller men, and a band of paid professional "prophets" sprang into existence and brought grave discredit on the movement, which soon became definitely separated from the Church. Localised at Pepuza, it sank lower and lower, becoming a "Puritan" sect of the most self-righteous order. It despised the historic Church and ministry, claimed an exclusive monopoly of the prophetic gifts of the Holy Ghost, denounced Churchmen as "carnal," and asserted that Montanists alone were "spiritual." All the most objectionable characteristics of the seventeenth-century sectaries in England were anticipated in them, and little by little they came back to the Gnostic standpoint against which their existence was originally a protest—the standpoint of an inner circle in religion, within which alone full knowledge of the truth was to be found.

Discredited in Asia, it rose to newness of life in Africa through the brilliant advocacy of Tertullian and the martyrdom of Perpetua and Felicitas. The former fell into schism, but the two latter continued to the end in the bosom of the Church, and so, in some measure, re-established for Montanism the reputation it had lost in Asia. Its chief tenets are set forth and defended by Tertullian in his "De Virginibus velandis," "De Corona Militis," "De fuga in persecutione," "De pudicitia," etc. They are summarised by St. Jerome in his letter to Marcella (xli.), a letter written in 385 showing that though condemned in the seventh Canon of the Council of Constantinople in 381, and refused the name of Christian, Montanists still flourished at the end of the fourth century and were full of proselytising zeal. They had tried, apparently, to make a convert of Marcella, and it was this attempt to win over one of his own children in the faith which drew from Jerome for her benefit a description of Montanist doctrine. From this document it seems that Montanism taught:

(1) *That Joel's prophecy* about the outpouring of the Spirit, which St. Peter declared to be there and

HERESIES AND SCHISMS

then fulfilled on the great day of Pentecost, was in reality fulfilled in Montanus.*

(2) *That Father, Son, and Holy Spirit are not Three Persons but One* (*i.e.* Montanists are followers of Sabellius, a presbyter of the Libyan Pentapolis in the early years of the third century, who " confounded the persons " of the Holy Trinity; in other words, Modalists who said that Christ is both Son and Father).

This charge, however, was not true of *all* Montanists. Proclus, *e.g.*, held orthodox views of the Holy Trinity, as did Felicitas and Perpetua. The followers of another Montanist leader, Aeschines, did hold the Sabellian view which Jerome attributes to them all.

(3) *That second marriages are adultery.*—The Church, says Jerome, while not encouraging them, yet allows them, because St. Paul bids the younger widows to marry. Tertullian confirms what Jerome says of the Montanists in this respect. In his " De exhortatione castitatis," chap. ix., he says, second marriages are adultery, " non aliud dicendum erit secundum matrimonium quam species stupri," and in his " De monogamia," chap. i., he says, " *unum* matrimonium novimus, sicut unum Deum," and in chap. ix., *ibid.*, that as all the laity are priests, they ought, like the clergy, to be monogamists.

(4) *That there are three Lents in the year.*—The *Catholic* Lent was originally of forty hours' duration—from 3 p.m. of Good Friday to early morning of Easter Day; during this time no food and no bath were

---

* *Cf.* Origen De princip. II. vii. 3 : Montanists " by entertaining unworthy ideas of His (Holy Ghost's) divinity have delivered themselves over to errors and deceits."

taken—the fast was complete and continuous. In Jerome's time it had been extended to forty *days* of partial and intermittent abstinence. He says the Montanists kept *three* Lents, but Tertullian, who would be better informed, says *two* (" De jejunio," chap. xv.).

(5) *That bishops are the lowest order of the ministry.*—" Cenonae " (aeconomi ?) being the middle rank, and the patriarchs of Pepuza the highest. This showed the Montanist contempt of institutional religion and of Catholic and historic Church and ministry.

(6) *That penitence is of doubtful efficacy.*—" They close the door of the Church on almost every offence, even the most trivial." Cf. Adv. John of Jerusalem, section 2 : " Montanus would hurl the fallen into the abyss that they may never rise again." Montanism forbade military service, shunned all heathen amusements, refused meats offered to idols, set up new fasts, and taught that not bishops but only " spiritual " men could give absolution. It made extreme austerity into an iron rule for all. It was this stern fanatic rigorism which made a Montanist of Tertullian.

(7) *Martyrdom of children:* a rumour which Jerome refused to believe.

(8) *That God first wished to save the world by Moses and the prophets*, but when this scheme failed, took to Himself a human body, and preaching under the form of the Son in Christ, underwent death for our salvation. This plan also not succeeding He descended by the Holy Spirit on Montanus, Prisca and Maximilla (xli. 4), two rich and high-born ladies whom Montanus used first to bribe and then to pervert many Churches (see cxxxiii. 4).

In spite of its later excesses Montanism remains

HERESIES AND SCHISMS

as a standing protest against the exclusion of enthusiasm and emotion from religion, and also against a too great laxity of discipline. It was, further, a reminder that prophecy must continue; not, however, as Montanus supposed, as the monopoly of a few favoured individuals, but as the possession of the whole Church of Christ.

(b) ORIGENISM

The second heresy, if such it can be called, with which Jerome came into collision was that known as Origenism. Though Origen, the great Alexandrian teacher, had passed away nearly a hundred years before Jerome's birth, his influence was in active operation in the closing decade of the fourth century.

In the letter of Epiphanius to John of Jerusalem, written in 394, and translated into Latin by Jerome, there is evidence of the hold which Origenism had taken even upon dignified clergy:

' doleo, et valde doleo, videns plurimos fratrum, *et eorum praecipue, qui professionem habent non minimam, et in gradum sacerdotii maximum pervenerunt*, ejus persuasionibus deceptos, et perversissima doctrina cibos factos esse diaboli."

Again in xcii., the Synodical letter of Theophilus to the Bishops of Palestine and of Cyprus, written in A.D. 400, it is stated:

" We have personally visited the monasteries of Nitria and find that the Origenistic heresy has made great ravages among them. It is accompanied by a strange fanaticism: men even maim themselves or cut out their tongues to show how they despise the

80 THE EPISTLES OF ST. JEROME

body. I find that some men of this kind have gone from Egypt into Syria and other countries where they speak against us and the truth."

Similarly in cxxvii. 9 Jerome, writing in 412, gives a vivid picture of Origenism in Rome:

" the muddy feet of heretics fouled the clear waters of the faith of Rome . . . next came the scandalous version (*i.e.* that published by Rufinus) of Origen's book ' On First Principles,' and that ' fortunate ' disciple (*i.e.* Macarius, a Roman Christian to whom Rufinus dedicated his volume), who would have been indeed fortunate had he never fallen in with such a master. Next followed the confutation set forth by my supporters which destroyed the cause of the Pharisees (Roman clerical supporters of Rufinus ?) and threw them into confusion. It was then that the holy Marcella, who had long held back lest she should be thought to act from party motives, threw herself into the breach, conscious that the faith of Rome, once praised by an Apostle, was now in danger, and that *this new heresy was drawing to itself not only priests and monks but also many of the laity, besides imposing on the* BISHOP * (Siricius), who fancied others as guileless as he was himself, and she publicly withstood its teachers, choosing to please God rather than men."

Thus Epiphanius, Theophilus, and Jerome all testify to the prevalence of Origenistic doctrines in their day.

It may next be asked what was the cause of the revival of interest in a teacher who had been dead

---

* His successor Anastasius, who condemned him, declared in 399 that he neither knew who Origen was nor what he had written.

HERESIES AND SCHISMS

one hundred and fifty years? The answer is to be found in the serious study of Scripture which was so characteristic a feature of Jerome's time, a study which he himself encouraged and fostered by every means in his power. This habit inevitably led the student to consult the greatest textual writer and interpreter of the Bible who had as yet been given to the Church, and those who, from the Hexapla and the commentaries, learned to admire him, were, by an easy transition, led on to study also his doctrinal writings and to sympathise more or less with his daring and dubious speculations.

Jerome, there is no doubt, had once a very real admiration for Origen. At late as 384 he commends him to Paula as a monument of industry whose prolific pen had well earned for him the title of Ἀδαμάντιος which Eusebius (H.E. vi. 14) had bestowed upon him. In this letter he even protests, in no measured terms, against the episcopal and other condemnations passed upon him.

" So you see the labours of this one man have excelled those of all previous writers. Greek or Latin—yet what reward have his exertions brought? He stands condemned by his bishop, Demetrius; only the bishops of Palestine, Arabia, Phœnicia, and Achaia dissenting. Imperial Rome consents to his condemnation, she convenes her Senate * to censure him, not as the rabid hounds who now pursue him cry, because of the novelty or heterodoxy of his doctrines, but because men could not tolerate the incomparable eloquence and knowledge which, when once he opened his lips, made others dumb " (xxxiii. 4).

* Word used loosely for a number of highly-placed people—*cf.* " Senate of Matrons," xliii. 3.

Similarly in xxxvi. he refers Damasus to Origen's writings for answers to questions he had asked about Noah's unclean animals and the Sacrament of Circumcision; while in lxxxi. 1 Rufinus declares that a " dear brother [*i.e.* Jerome] had said that Origen was second only to the Apostles as a teacher of the Church in wisdom and knowledge, and that while in his other books he had surpassed all former writers, in dealing with the Song of Songs he had surpassed himself."

These quotations are sufficient to show the spirit of Jerome's earlier attitude to Origen. Presently, however, that attitude is entirely changed, outwardly at any rate, though probably his inward feelings and convictions with regard to him were but little modified by time or circumstances. An anti-Origenist movement arises among the monks of Egypt which the Bishop of Alexandria (Theophilus) first opposed, but finally supported. Jerome's bishop, John of Jerusalem, was an Origenist and so was his old friend Rufinus, who had a Monastery on the Mount of Olives. On the other hand, Epiphanius, Bishop of Salamis, whom Jerome regarded as a saint, took the side of Theophilus, and Jerome felt himself compelled to do the same. Consequently there is a remarkable change of tone in the latter's later references to Origen. He is acutely sensitive as to his reputation for orthodoxy, and when he became conscious of the force of the anti-Origenist movement and of the widespread determination to brand him as a heretic, he does not hesitate to range himself against him. Writing to Theophilus in 399 (lxxxii. 2) he claims :

" I neither rend the Church nor separate myself from the communion of the Fathers. From my cradle

HERESIES AND SCHISMS

I have been reared on Catholic milk, and no one can be a better Churchman than one who has never been a heretic."

In the following year he assures Oceanus and Pammachius, " I will hold fast in my old age the faith wherein I was born again in my boyhood " (lxxxiv. 8). It was this burning desire to pose before the world as a Churchman of unquestionable orthodoxy which explains his change of front and his vehement letter to Vigilantius protesting against the charge of pro-Origenist leanings. More violent still is his language in lxxxiv. 3:

" His (Origen's) doctrines are poisonous, they are unknown to the Holy Scriptures—nay more, they contradict them. I have read Origen, I repeat, I have read him; and if it is a crime to read him, I admit my guilt, indeed these Alexandrian writings have emptied my purse. If you will believe me I have never been an Origenist; if you *will* not believe me, I have now ceased to be one."

In the same epistle he pleads in explanation of his altered attitude, " I have praised the commentator but not the theologian; the man of intellect but not the believer; the philosopher but not the apostle "— he had but approved of him " as Cyprian approved Tertullian " (lxxxiv. 2)—a passage with which may be compared lxxxii. 7 : " While I have always allowed Origen his great merit as an interpreter and critic of the Scriptures, I have invariably denied the truth of his doctrines." In lxxxv. 4 he again pleads, " I merely repudiate his objectionable dogmas." In all these statements Jerome seems to be protesting too much, and there is little doubt that a good deal of his early admiration for Origen survived to the end of his life, though he dares no longer to give full expression to it. It is very probable, also, that he came to realise that not all the Alexandrian's writings were suitable for uninstructed and indiscriminate use, for he asks pointedly in lxxxii. 7 : " Is it I that let him loose upon the crowd ? " ("Num quid ego in turbam mitto Origenem ? ")

Jerome's epistles, therefore, illustrate the widespread diffusion of Origenism, especially in the East, and the bitter feuds it engendered between John of Jerusalem and Epiphanius of Cyprus, between Theophilus of Alexandria and Chrysostom of Constantinople, between Jerome himself and his former friend, Rufinus. They also throw light on the nature of the heresy itself. The letters most useful for this purpose are :

(a) li. from Epiphanius to John of Jerusalem.

(b) xcii. the synodic letter of Theophilus to the bishops of Palestine and Cyprus.

(c) cxxiv. to Avitus.

(d) The letter to Pammachius against John of Jerusalem, especially sections 7 and 17.

From these four documents may be formed a fairly complete summary of Origen's distinctive doctrines.

(1) That Christ is inferior to the Father and superior to the Holy Ghost. The Son cannot see the Father, neither can the Spirit see the Son.

(2) That Christ is only relatively good. Compared with us He is truth, compared with the Father He is falsehood.

HERESIES AND SCHISMS

(3) That Christ's kingdom will come to an end.

(4) That there is nothing perfect even in heaven; some angels are faulty and feed on Jewish sacraments.

(5) That the stars are conscious of their own movements and demons know the future by their courses.

(6) That sun, moon, and stars are the souls of what were once reasonable and incorporeal creatures, and that though now subject to vanity they shall be delivered from the bondage of corruption into the glorious liberty of the children of God.

(7) That magic, if real, is not evil.

(8) That Christ suffered once for man and will suffer again for demons, in which case He will Himself become a demon.

(9) That one who is now a human being may in another world become a demon; an Archangel a devil; and *vice versa*.

(10) That bodily substances will be highly rarefied or else pass away altogether at the end of all things and leave us incorporeal.

(11) That hell-fire is the fire of conscience.

(12) That after many ages and one restitution of all things, it will be the same for Gabriel as for the devil, for Paul as for Caiaphas, and for virgins as for prostitutes (lxxxiv. 7).

(13) That there is a plurality of worlds, a new one beginning each time the old one comes to an end.

(14) That there is a transmigration of souls (which may explain " Jacob have I loved but Esau have I hated ").

(15) That souls were once angels in heaven, but for having sinned have been cast down to earth and

confined in bodies as in tombs (in support of this theory Origen points to the words for corpse in Greek and Latin πτῶμα from πίπτω, cadaver from cado).

(16) That Satan will ultimately be restored to heaven.

(17) That Adam lost the image of God at the Fall.

Besides teaching the above doctrines, he is accused (Adv. John of Jerusalem 7) of so allegorising the early chapters of Genesis as to divest them of all historical meaning: *e.g.* the coats of skins with which Adam and Eve clothed themselves are but human bodies; the trees of Paradise are angels; the rivers are heavenly virtues; the waters above the firmament are holy and supernal essences, while those above and below the earth are demoniacal essences. Also he is said to deny the Resurrection of the flesh.

Alexandria may be described as the home of Allegorism, and, in adopting it, Origen was but using a weapon which was familiar both to his contemporaries and to former generations whether Jewish, Christian, or heathen. The method had its origin in the conviction that, while the venerable antiquity of certain books gives them a sanctity in the eyes of the reader, their contents are not always such as to inspire sufficient reverence. The plain literal narrative is therefore assumed to conceal a profounder meaning at which the author only hinted in types and symbols. The poems of Homer were thus treated by Greek philosophers; the Iliad was but the story of the soul battling against evil, the Odyssey a picture of man tossed about on the seas of passion and pleasure.

Philo was the first, apparently, to apply the system to the Jewish Scriptures, while a very early

Christian document—the so-called "Epistle of Barnabas"—allegorises even the 318 servants of Abraham—the numeral letters of ten and eight being I and H—must suggest Jesus ; and because the Cross was that by which we are to find grace, therefore the writer of Genesis adds three hundred, the note of which is T—wherefore by two letters he signifies Jesus, and by the third His Cross. It was, therefore, no new tool which Origen took up. Allegoric interpretation was the accepted scientific method of his day, and however wanting it might be in historic sense, and however weak on its apologetic side, it is well to remember that it was Ambrose's allegorical sermons at Milan which first made Augustine think seriously of the Old Testament. And though its interpretations might sometimes sound fantastic, they were hardly less objectionable than the crude rigid literalism of the Jew, and they at least asserted the principle that the words of God—though spoken on some definite historic occasion—are not thereby exhausted of their meaning, but retain an eternal significance.

The book "Περὶ 'Αρχῶν" or "De Principiis" was the work round which the Origenistic controversy mainly raged and in which most of his speculative doctrines are to be found. It has been called "the most remarkable production of ante-Nicene times." Written when Origen was only thirty and still a layman it won for him (says Dr. Kidd, "History of the Church," vol. i. pp. 410–11) the rank of the first great philosophic or systematic theologian ; "only fragments of it remain in the Greek original, but the whole is preserved in the Latin translation of Rufinus, who, however, took considerable liberties with the text." It was "written not for the simple believer but for the scholar . . . the first three books contain the exposition of a Christian philosophy, gathered round the three ideas of God, the world, and the rational soul; and the last gives the basis of it in the Scriptures." It has three merits which no candid opponent could deny; he never slurs a difficulty, never dogmatises, never consciously departs from the teaching of Scripture (*ibid.*, p. 412).

Jerome has stated Origen's doctrine of the subordination of Christ in too one-sided a fashion. The subordination he taught was not of rank or time but of thought. In any right thinking about God, the Father must come first. Origen's enemies fastened on his subordinationist language and ignored his clear recognition of coeternity and coequality. As Dr. Kidd observes (*ibid.*, p. 423):

"after all, Origen's subordinationism was purely scriptural. It was simply explanatory of such texts as 'My Father is greater than I'; 'That they may know Thee, the only true God'; and 'None is good save one, that is God'; and the dominant text in his mind is the last."

(c) PELAGIANISM

The third and last heresy with which Jerome came into contact was that associated with the name of Pelagius, though it was not Jerome but Augustine who was its chief opponent. Pelagius, a native of Britain, probably of South-West Wales, was a monk and a layman, a man of high character whom, in an age of fiercest controversy, no breath of slander or

HERESIES AND SCHISMS

scandal ever assailed; a scholar, too, of no mean attainments, well acquainted both with Greek and Latin. Arriving in Rome in the closing years of the fourth century, he soon came under the influence of the Syrian Rufinus, who had brought with him the opinions of Theodore of Mopsuestia, opinions which, in the main, were adopted by Pelagius and were first given by him to the world in a commentary on the Epistle to the Romans. They found in him a fruitful soil because they corresponded with his experience of the religious life of Rome. He had noticed with sorrow the laxity which, generally speaking, characterises the Christian community in the capital in the years immediately preceding the Gothic invasions, and had attributed it to a defective realisation of their responsibility to God for their actions. But it was the Augustinian doctrine which drove him to take up, with vigour, the extreme teaching with which his name became identified. Such a prayer, *e.g.*, as that in the tenth book of the "Confessions": "Lord, Thou hast commanded continence; give what Thou commandest and command what Thou wilt," seemed to him fatal to moral effort and false in its theology. There was no need to pray "give" when the power had already been bestowed as part of the original endowment of the race. In his anxiety to counteract the fatalism of Augustine, he gathered round him a band of disciples of whom Caelestius was the chief, who continued to propagate Pelagianism in Rome till the Gothic advance compelled them to leave the capital and to settle (1) in Sicily, and (2) in Africa.

The principal tenets of Pelagius were four in

number. Starting from a Stoic conception of human nature he asserted :

(1) *The unqualified freedom of the will.* In every free action there were, he said, three elements— " posse," " velle," " esse "—of these the first, *i.e.* the power to choose evil or good, belongs by right to God, who bestows it on man at his birth; the other two—to desire and to be—rest with man because they have their source in his will.

(2) *The possibility of living without sin.* The human will, according to Pelagius, had never undergone weakening or impoverishment and was quite equal to the strain of living a sinless life.

(3) *There is no " Original Sin."* No inherited inclination to evil; to admit such a doctrine was Manichaeism very thinly disguised. If man's first parents did him any harm at all, it was only by setting a bad example.

(4) *There was no such thing as a Fall.*

All sorts of consequences subversive of the Christian Faith followed from these conclusions. New definitions were required both of grace and of the means of grace. Grace was no longer the divine supernatural help which was man's daily indispensable need, it was his possession of reason and freewill conferred upon him at the Creation and constituting his superiority to the beasts—a possession fortified since the Christian era by the example of Jesus Christ. It was difficult to see what place there was for prayer in a Christian's life if Pelagius' teaching were true, or what exactly was the use of Confirmation and the Eucharist, or indeed what necessity there was for man's redemption at all. Baptism, on which he insisted,

HERESIES AND SCHISMS

was not, in the case of children at any rate, " for the remission of sins."

It was this last point which led to the condemnation of Caelestius at the Council of Carthage in 411-12. When confronted with the everywhere established custom of Infant Baptism he could not deny it; nor could he claim that it was administered in their case otherwise than as with adults, viz. " unto remission of sins." The sin of infants could not be an act of will—it must therefore be a sin of nature, an admission which implies both a Fall and Original Sin.

Immediately after the condemnation of Caelestius, Augustine began in sermons and treatises to vigorously attack the Pelagian doctrines, continuing and developing the argument from the Church's practice of Infant Baptism.

In the Church of Christ there are no forms for form's sake. Her ordinances are few and simple, superior to those of the Jews because they are not mere ceremonies but also sacraments with their special grace. If, then, baptism confers an inward spiritual grace, infants who are brought to it must have a spiritual need. What is the need ? If they do not suffer from inherited sinfulness, we ought to say to their sponsors " take those innocents away," instead of " suffer the little children to come unto Me."

It is impossible here to follow in detail the course of Augustine's many anti-Pelagian writings or to track the heresy through its chequered career in Palestine, Africa, Britain, and Italy, or to do more than mention its reprobation at Rome by Innocent in 417, its ill-considered approval by Zosimus in the same year, its subsequent condemnation by the same

Pontiff and by the Emperor in 418; the rise of semi-Pelagianism, *i.e.* the denial of the necessity of grace as prevenient to the first motions of conversion, the excesses of Augustinianism, and the final acceptance of a Catholic doctrine of Grace at the Council of Orange in 529. Suffice it to say that there the main Augustinian teachings were adopted by the Church, viz. the Fall, Original Sin, the need of Grace as originating, assisting, sustaining the life of the soul. The crude and ruthless excesses of Augustine were passed over in discreet and significant silence, viz. predestination, the view of humanity as a "mass of perdition," the denial of salvation to unbaptised infants, and the irresistibility and indefectibility of grace.

Jerome, though not exactly a protagonist was a combatant in this campaign. When Orosius, with documents from Augustine, arrived in Palestine in 415 he found him in the thick of the controversy. Pelagius was then in the country and had incurred the fierce hostility of Jerome (who called him " Rufinus resurrected ") by writing to Demetrias a letter full of his peculiar tenets, and by cultivating friendly relations with his old enemy, John of Jerusalem. The Synod of Diospolis, however, in 415 accepted the assurances of Pelagius and acquitted him in the absence of his accusers, Heros of Arles and Lazarus of Aix, though it condemned the heresy of Caelestius. The result was a deep disappointment to Jerome who, in letter cxxxviii., had branded Pelagius as Catiline and Caelestius as Lentulus. In epistle cxxxiii. he traces the chief Pelagian doctrines to the " poisonous teaching of all the heretics," especially to that of the

HERESIES AND SCHISMS

Manichaeans, Priscillian, Origen, Basilides, which in its turn was derived from Pythagoras and Zeno. He pours scorn on their belief that it is possible to eradicate vice merely by meditating upon and practising virtue. To maintain such a doctrine is to forget that man is body as well as soul, and to substitute simple wishes for sound instruction. The principal theory of Pelagius, the perfectibility of human nature, is refuted by all experience and by the lives even of the saints, none of whom was perfect. The qualifying sentence, " but not without the grace of God," by which Pelagius sought to disarm criticism, is contemptuously dismissed by Jerome because by " grace " Pelagius meant the Divine gift of freewill bestowed once for all at the Creation, a definition which removed the necessity of prayer and of all other external helps, for it were useless to ask God for what is already in our own hands.

Again, says Jerome, Pelagians declare that a man may be perfect and without sin if only he wills it, yet it is absurd to put forward this contention and then, when challenged, fail to point to one single sinless person.

" Moreover, if we ask them who they are whom they regard as sinless, they seek to veil the truth by a new subterfuge. They do not, they say, profess that men are or have been without sin; they only maintain that it is *possible* for them so to be. Remarkable teachers, truly! to maintain that a thing *may* be which on their own showing never has been! "

And if his argument suggests Manichaeism, which holds that there are two natures diverse from one another, and that the evil nature cannot be changed, Jerome is satisfied to refer his cavillers to St. Paul and to shelter himself behind Galatians v. 17 : " caro enim desiderat contra Spiritum et Spiritus contra carnem, et haec invicem sibi adversantur," etc. And if it seems to deny freewill altogether to maintain that man needs the help of God moment by moment, Jerome asks Pelagius pointedly :

" Do you or do you not wish to be free from sin ? If yes, why on your own principle do you not carry out your desire ? If you do not wish to be sinless you are a despiser of God's commandments and therefore a sinner " (cxxxiii. 11).

Having placed Pelagius on the horns of this dilemma Jerome next accuses him of having one doctrine for the outside world and another for his own esoteric disciples—a just charge—for, in his letter to Demetrias, Pelagius (sections 3 and 8) says, that philosophers before Christ had lived perfectly, and St. Augustine in " De natura et gratia," section 42, says he had prepared lists of Scripture characters who, in his opinion, had never sinned.

It is comparatively easy to understand the positions taken up in this controversy by Pelagius and Augustine, positions to be traced back in large measure to their own very different experiences of life. The former seems to have led the quiet, uneventful monotonous life of the cloister and of the study, and to such a man (as Harnack points out in his " History of Dogma," vol. v. p. 170) goodness appears to be no very difficult matter. Their own will rather than the hand of God seems to keep men

HERESIES AND SCHISMS

in the narrow way. Hence the inconsistencies of the nominal Christians of Rome who pleaded, as an excuse for themselves, the weakness of the flesh, were to Pelagius culpable in the extreme, being easily preventable by the unaided effort of will.

But the outlook of Augustine, who had mixed freely with the world and was deeply stained by his contact with it, was necessarily of quite another character. He had sinned grossly and repeatedly, he had been brought to repentance: what was he but a brand plucked from the burning, a standing miracle of grace, a living illustration of the text: "What hast thou that thou didst not receive?" To such a man the human will was nothing, and salvation the work exclusively of a merciful God. As Dr. Bright puts it in his introduction to the "Anti-Pelagian treatises of Augustine," pp. l.–li. :

"Year after year he must have pondered more deeply the wonderful experiences of that earlier time, when, as he believed, a Divine purpose of grace had pursued him through his wild youth and restless manhood, until it conquered him under the fig-tree at Milan. And amid these musings, the awe which lay so deep in his piety, would root in his mind the thought 'in God's moral realm He must be the sole mover; He cannot allow His subjects to limit His action or cross His design.' Grace, intensely contemplated, would fill the whole mental scene. . . . His studies of St. Paul's epistles would more and more seem to require this conclusion, to shape in his mind the idea of a Will Absolute, which, out of a "mass" of souls, all alike deserving perdition on account even of Original Sin, selected a minority to be vessels of Divine mercy, and abandoned the majority as vessels of Divine wrath, without any regard in either case to foreseen moral character. And in the case of souls predestinated or elected to salvation, he came to hold that grace so bent the will to its own pleasure, as literally to make it respond and obey; in a word, that grace was irresistible and therefore indefectible; for being irresistible it must needs achieve its object. These beliefs . . . gained systematic solidity and distinctness in the course of his battle with Pelagianism. Intent above all things on magnifying the Divine sovereignty he practically forgot the complexity of the problem . . . and failed to do justice to the human element, in the mysterious process of man's salvation."

Jerome's position in this controversy is much more difficult to define and understand. He was not a predestinarian like Augustine, and there are passages in his anti-Pelagian dialogues which seem to suggest that his standpoint is more or less that of a synergist or semi-pelagian—such as Vitalis or Cassian some ten years later, who both ascribe the initiative in good to man and its consummation to God (see Aug. Ep. ccxvii. 1, and Cassian Collatio xiii. 8). The sections in Jerome's anti-Pelagian works which support this view of his attitude to the question are:

Adv. Pelag. i. 5:

"Have you not read that it is not of him that willeth nor of him that runneth, but of God that showeth mercy"? (Romans ix. 16). "From this we understand that to will and to run is ours, but the carrying into effect our willing and running pertains to the mercy of God, and is so effected that on the one hand in willing and running freewill is preserved; and on the other, in consummating our willing and running, everything is left to the power of God."

HERESIES AND SCHISMS

Similarly in ii. 5:

"'Her sins which are many are forgiven her, for she loved much'; this shows that the doing what we wish does not depend merely upon our own power, but upon the assistance which God in His mercy gives to our will."

Or iii. 1:

"Let me tell you that baptism condones past offences and does not preserve righteousness in the time to come; the keeping of that is dependent on toil and industry as well as earnestness, and above all, on the mercy of God. It is ours to ask, to Him it belongs to bestow what we ask; ours it is to begin, His it is to finish; ours to offer what we can, His to fulfil what we cannot perform."

Jerome had no part in the Synod of Diospolis, yet he somehow drew down upon himself the fierce wrath of the Pelagians who actually attacked and nearly destroyed his monasteries. Possibly he may once have shown them a certain degree of sympathy which he afterwards withdrew from fear of suspected orthodoxy and under pressure from Orosius and Augustine. If this be true, the animosity of the Pelagians is explained and Jerome's attitude to them is but a repetition of his earlier attitude to the Origenists.

VII

DOCTRINE AND PRACTICE

HOLY Communion.—There is very little to be found in these epistles as to the Eucharistic doctrine of St. Jerome's day, but that considerable importance was attached to the Lord's Supper is clear from a question and answer of the writer himself in xlviii. 15 : " Which is the more important, to pray or to receive Christ's body ? Surely to receive Christ's body."

In xlvi. 2 Paula and Eustochium, writing to Marcella, and doubtless reflecting Jerome's opinion which, in its turn, would echo the orthodox doctrine of the Church, declare Melchizedek's offering of bread and wine to be a type of the Lord's Supper.

In li. 1 Epiphanius states that Jerome and Vincent were " unwilling to offer the sacrifices permitted to their rank and to labour in that part of their calling which *more than any other ministers to the salvation of Christians.*"

In cxlvi. 1 he speaks of bishops and presbyters as those " at whose prayers the Body and Blood of Christ are produced."

In cxiv. 2 he praises Theophilus of Alexandria for insisting on the reverent care of the sacred vessels which ought to be venerated as the Body and Blood themselves !

DOCTRINE AND PRACTICE

In lxxi. 6 addressing Lucinius, a wealthy Spaniard, who had asked him whether he ought to receive the Eucharist daily according to the reported custom of the Churches of Rome and Spain, Jerome answers much after the manner of Gregory to Augustine, that local Church customs if not opposed to the faith, are to be observed as handed down, the use of one Church is not to be annulled merely because it is in conflict with that of another. Each province may follow its own inclination.

Spain, Africa, and Constantinople seem at this time to have had a daily Eucharist, but at Rome, according to Socrates (H.E. v. 22), there was no celebration on Saturdays. In the Anti-Pelagian Dialogues iii. 15, Jerome seems to imply that a daily Eucharist was the practice of the Church: " Our Lord so instructed His Apostles that *daily* at the sacrifice of His Body believers might make bold to say, ' Our Father which art in Heaven.' " *

Augustine in his " De Sermone Domini in Monte," ii. 26, speaks of a daily Eucharist as his own custom and that of the African Church.

Nicetas, Bishop of Remesiana in Serbia, says a daily Eucharist was the custom there (" De diversis appellationibus," section 1).

In cxxv. 20, Exuperius, Bishop of Toulouse, is said to have carried about the sacred bread in a wicker basket and the sacred wine in a glass.

In lxxxii. 2, Jerome insists to Theophilus that a necessary condition of worthy reception is to be in charity with all men :

* N.B. the sacrificial language applied to the Eucharist by Jerome.

"I know nothing of a peace that is without love or of a Communion that is without peace . . . if we may not offer gifts that are our own unless we are at peace with our brothers, how much less can we receive the Body of Christ if we cherish enmity in our hearts? How can I conscientiously approach Christ's Eucharist and answer the 'Amen,' if I doubt the charity of him who ministers it?"

Earlier in his life Jerome seems to have attached a special value to the Eucharist at Rome, for in xvii. 2 he says, "Quicumque extra hanc domum, agnum comederit, profanus est."

Apparently, too, at Rome in his day both reservation and non-communicating attendance were unknown, for he writes in xlviii. 15: "Scio Romæ hanc esse consuetudinem ut fideles semper Christi corpus accipiant."

With regard both to Baptism and the Lord's Supper, it may be said that the doctrine underlying them was in the fourth and fifth centuries essentially what it had been before.* No doubt Christian experience and the struggle with paganism and heresy tended to produce explanations, but the main thought was always that of life bestowed and life maintained. . . .

"The great contribution of the age to the doctrine of the Sacraments is the view that in a real sense they continue the process of the Incarnation. Human nature first became divine in the person of Christ by union with the Divine Word, and subsequently and repeatedly in the person of the individual believer through union with Christ in the Sacraments. This

* Stewart, "Cambridge Mediæval History," pp. 588-9.

DOCTRINE AND PRACTICE 101

is the teaching of both East and West as represented by Hilary and Gregory of Nyssa. As in Baptism the soul is joined to Christ through faith, so in the Eucharist is the body, being transformed by the Eucharistic food, joined with the Body of the Lord. Thus the special purpose of the Incarnation, viz. the deification of man, is being constantly fulfilled. The language in which this noble conception is expressed, especially in the East, tends to encourage a superstitious reverence for the outward symbols, which the Greek fathers frequently have occasion to correct " (*ibid.*, p. 590).

Baptism.—There is not much in these letters to throw light on the view of Christian baptism held by the Church at the time, or on the ritual and practice connected with its administration, but it may be inferred from xvii. 3 that a " form of sound words " had to be repeated by every candidate for the rite, for Jerome complains to the presbyter Marcus that every day the Syrian solitaries ask him for his profession of faith as if he had not already made it when regenerated in baptism (" quotidie exposcor fidem quasi sine fide renatus sum "). It seems, too, from Adv. John of Jerusalem 13, that public lectures on the Holy Trinity were wont to be delivered to those about to be baptised during the forty days of Lent.

In lxix. 5 he speaks of it as an " efficacious rite "—in (6) of the same letter he maintains that the infant world, produced by the Spirit moving on the waters at the Creation, is a type of the Christian child lifted out of the laver of baptism. Again in lxix. 7 he says, " all sins are drowned in the laver." Augustine in a letter to Jerome (cxxx., Migne) about the origin of the soul assumes throughout the damnation of unbaptised infants especially in this sentence : " Christi Ecclesia nec parvulos homines recentissime natos a damnatione credit, nisi per gratiam nominis Christi quam in suis sacramentis commendavit posse liberari."

Jerome believed that baptism meant regeneration, membership of Christ and the forgiveness of sins, for in Anti-Pelag. iii. 15 he writes :

" They rise from the baptismal font, and by being born again and incorporated into our Lord and Saviour fulfil thus what is written of them—' Blessed are they whose iniquities are forgiven and whose sins are covered.' "

Mr. Stewart (" Cambridge Mediaeval History," p. 589) well sums up the teaching of the time on this subject :

" The water of Baptism did not invite speculation to the same degree as did the bread and wine, and their relation to the Body and Blood of Christ. Not that Baptism was ever regarded merely as a ceremony of initiation ; it was the fear of losing, through postbaptismal sin, the grace conveyed by Baptism that in our period kept many from the font. Other causes such as negligence, reluctance to forgo the world, and various fancies and superstitions, combined to render Baptism, as in Constantine's case, the completion rather than the commencement of Christian life. Such delay was not the intention of the Church, and the necessity of checking slackness, together with the Western doctrine of prevenient grace helping the first step Godward, brought about a strict insistence on the necessity of Baptism, and a readiness in the West, at least, to allow the Baptism of heretics, provided the right form of words was used. But both wisdom

DOCTRINE AND PRACTICE

and generosity were shown by the refusal to tie down the operation of the Holy Spirit to ritual action, and by the admission of faith, repentance, or martyrdom, as substitutes for formal Baptism when this could not be had."

From the Dialogue against the Luciferians, section 8, it seems that the following traditional practices had in Jerome's time acquired the force of the written law of the Church, viz.: (1) Dipping the head three times in the laver. (2) After leaving the water, tasting mingled milk and honey in representation of infancy.

From ditto (9) it appears that laymen might, and frequently did, baptise. Priests and deacons might not do so without the licence of the bishop.

The effect of Baptism is described in ditto (22):

" As the raven is sent forth from the Ark but does not return and afterwards the dove announces peace to the earth—so in the Church's baptism, that most unclean bird, the devil, is expelled, and the dove of the Holy Spirit announces peace to our earth."

Relics.—The importance attached at this time to relics is evidenced to some extent in the epistles, though the question is more fully considered in the treatise against Vigilantius.

In cix. 1 he says clearly that the Church honours, but does not worship them.

In cxviii. 4 he commends Julian, a Dalmatian nobleman, because forty days after the death of his daughters he put off his mourning for a white robe in order to attend the dedication of a martyr's bones —" unconcerned for a bereavement which was the concern of the whole city and anxious only to rejoice at a martyr's triumph."

That they were made much of at this time—more than Jerome allows in cix. 1—may be seen from the life of Chrysostom, who in 398 organised a procession by night from the Great Church at Constantinople to the Church of St. Thomas in Drypia, nine miles off, to translate the relics of some saints. The Empress Eudoxia, robed in purple and wearing the diadem, followed the reliquary all the way on foot, touching the cloth that covered it, so as to miss no spiritual benefit; next day the Emperor Arcadius visited it and made adoration. It was such practices which stirred the wrath of Vigilantius—the practice of costly shrines and silken wrappings for relics, of offering them to be kissed, of praying to them, of vigils, of tapers and alleged miracles at the tombs of martyrs (Adv. Vigil. 4, 9, 10).

Pilgrimages.—The growth of this habit is described by Jerome with characteristic hyperbole in cviii. 8, where he asks : " What race of men is there which does not send pilgrims to the holy places ? " Paula and Eustochium in xlvi. 9 insist that education is incomplete without seeing Jerusalem, and the extent to which the practice prevailed is indicated in the section following :

" Every man of note in Gaul hastens thither, the Briton no sooner makes progress in religion than he leaves the setting sun in quest of a spot of which he knows only through Scripture and common report. Need we recall the Armenians, the Persians, the Indians, the Ethiopians ? Or those of our neighbour, Egypt, so rich in monks ? Of Pontus, of Cappadocia,

DOCTRINE AND PRACTICE

of Caele-Syria and Mesopotamia and the teeming East ? "

As this statement comes from Paula and Eustochium it may be accepted with less hesitation than if it had proceeded from Jerome—and their admission should be noted that Christ's presence cannot be localised and that His Kingdom is within us (xlvi. 10). Similarly, Jerome himself is fully alive to the fact that access to heaven is as easy from Britain as from Jerusalem (lviii. 3). " I do not presume to limit God's omnipotence or to restrict to a narrow strip of earth Him Whom the heavens cannot contain " (*ibid.*). Gregory of Nyssa writes to the same effect : " change of place does not make God nearer " (de Eunt. Hieros. ii. 1087)—so also does Chrysostom—" It is not necessary to make a pilgrimage, or travel to distant lands, or to undergo dangers and toils—but only to have the will " (Hom. I. in Ep. ad Philem). Yet in spite of such sayings, the belief became more and more general that particular saints helped and protected particular places and people, and that God was more easily to be propitiated at the shrines of the martyrs than elsewhere.

Other points of interest in Jerome's letters may be briefly mentioned :

(1) The practice of making *the sign of the Cross;* the dying Paula, *e.g.*, makes it (see cviii. 21).

(2) *Observance of Church seasons and saints' days,* *e.g.* Lent (cvii. 10) and St. Peter's Day (xxxi. 2).

(3) *Prayers of the departed for the living.* Jerome tells Paula he is confident the dead Blesilla will

intercede for him (xxxix. 6). In cviii. 34 he asks the deceased Paula to aid him in his old age with her prayers. In xiv. 3 he tells Heliodorus that after he has passed away he (Heliodorus) will intercede for Jerome who had urged him forward on the path of victory; in lxxv. 2 he assures the widowed Theodora that her late husband Lucinius will look down upon her from on high and support her in her struggle.

VIII

CONCLUSION

DEAN FREMANTLE in his "Prolegomena to Jerome" says (p. xxxiii.) truly enough:

"His writings contain the whole spirit of the Church of the Middle Ages, its Monasticism, its contrast of sacred things with profane, its credulity and superstition, its value for relics, its subjection to hierarchical authority, its dread of heresy, its passion for pilgrimages."

But after all it is the Vulgate which was his crowning achievement and his greatest contribution to the Church of Christ. In it his varied gifts are seen to most advantage, for, as a translator of the Bible, he shows a capacity, a caution, a patience, an independence of judgment, a diligence and a critica acumen which he nowhere else displays. For evidence of some of these qualities the famous "Prologus Galeatus" is sufficient where he defies the "mad dogs who bark and rave" at his work; so also is his firm and clear discrimination between the Old Testament and the Apocrypha and his unflinching resolve in spite of the Council of Nicaea, to class the book of Judith in the latter. The Vulgate is indeed his masterpiece, between which and his epistles there is a great gulf fixed as regards literary and spiritual worth. It is impossible to read even a few pages of his correspondence without realising its highly rhetorical character and that the writer is allowing to run riot that forensic training which he, like so many other fathers of the Church, had received.

An artist in words must be necessarily scrutinised with strictness and suspicion, and his sonorous sentences must be critically sifted and compared with other trustworthy testimony before they can be accepted at their face value. Jerome's love of literary effect, his brusque Johnsonian dogmatism, his unscrupulous invective (*e.g.* against Vigilantius or Onasus of Segeste (xl. 3)), his credulity and superstition (*e.g.* 1 " de muliere septies percussa "), all impress the reader with the need of caution and reserve. He has the nervous sensitiveness and irritability of the scholar-recluse, and the monk's tendency to flights of imagination.

There can be little doubt, *e.g.*, that his account of the fall of Rome is much exaggerated : " Urbs inclyta et Romani imperii caput uno hausta est incendio . . . in cineres ac favillas sacrae quondam ecclesiae conciderunt " (cxxviii. 4); whereas we know from Orosius' History vii. and other sources, that Alaric refrained from destroying churches. As Sir S. Dill conjectures (p. 307) : " The warm imagination and vehement rhetoric of St. Jerome have probably deepened the colours of the tragic tales of massacre and sacrilege which reached him." Yet he has bequeathed, to later generations, portraits of contemporary life both pagan and Christian, but especially Christian, which no student of the period can presume to ignore. His vivid pictures of the fashionable

CONCLUSION

clerical fop with his lusts and his legacy hunts, of the real and nominal monks and virgins, are evidently drawn from life ; his description of the learned ladies on the Aventine immortalises a unique chapter in the history of the Church, while his sketches of the ascetic movement are essential to any record of the fourth and fifth centuries. Jerome, in fact, shows in their beginnings three institutions on which the Christianity of the Middle Ages took its stand, viz. the Vulgate, the Monastery, the Papacy, a triumvirate which reigned and ruled for more than a millennium; he shows, too, a Church which, outwardly victorious over heathenism and heresy, was still sowing the seeds of internal corruption and needing continually to pray : " In all time of our wealth, good Lord deliver us."

INDEX

Aeschines, 77
Agapetae, 8
Akiba, Rabbi, 29
Alaric, 108
Alexandria, 13–18
Algasia, 22
Allegorism, 86–87
Altar of Victory, 70
Altars, studded with jewels, 6
Ambrose, 14, 17, 59, 87
Ambrosiaster, 10, 11
Ammianus Marcellinus, 9, 49, 54
Anastasius, 80
Anchorites, 42
Antioch, see of, 56, 61, 73
Antony, 38, 39
Apocrypha, 33, 107
"Apostolic Church Order," 17, 18
Applause in church, 3, 4
Aquila, 31
Arcadius, 104
Aristotle, 69
Arius, 16
Arles, Council of, 11
Asceticism, 38–53
Asella, 44
Athanasius, 18, 41
Attalus, 70
Augustine of Hippo, 4, 5, 6, 9, 13, 23, 30, 31, 35, 36, 87, 88, 89, 91, 92, 94, 95, 96, 99, 101

Baptism, 90, 101–103
—— of infants, 91
Baraninas, 32
Barnabas, epistle of St., 87
Bede, Venerable, 24

Bigg, Dr. C., 14
Bingham, 14
Bishops, 12
Blesilla, 22, 44, 49, 105
Bonosus, 47
Brahmans, 48
Bright, Dr. W., 95
Buddha, 48

Caelestius, 89, 91
"Cambridge Mediaeval History," vol. i., 6, 12, 16, 18, 53, 57, 65
Canon of Scripture, 37, 57
Canons of Hippolytus, 17
—— of Nicaea, 4
—— of Sardica, 61
Carthage, Council of, 91
Cassian, 53, 96
Cellia, 39
Cenonae, 78
Chalcis, desert of, 41
Chrysostom, St., 4, 5, 8, 65, 84, 104
——, St., "de Sacerdotio," 6
Church, corruption of, 50
——, progress of, 64–72
Clergy in Jerome's day, 1–19
——, morals of, 1–10
——, orders of, 10–19
Coenobites, 42, 43
Confirmation, 90
Constantine I., 5, 66
——, "Exemptiones" of, 5
Constantius, 66
Cornelius, 60
Cross, sign of, 105
Cucurbita, 20, 36
Cyprian, 17, 59, 83
Cyprian (presbyter), 22

INDEX

Damasus, 3, 20, 27, 28, 55, 56, 57, 58, 59, 63, 82
Dardanus, 23
Deacons, 11, 12
Decius, 60
De Civitate Dei, 31, 48
Demetrias, 46, 92, 94
Demetrius, 18
Dill, Sir S., 8, 48, 49, 108
Dionysius of Corinth, 60
Diospolis, Synod of, 92, 97
Doctrine, 98–106

Eleusinian mysteries, 70
Epiphanius, 14, 19, 73, 79, 80, 82, 84
Eucharist, 11, 90, 98–101
Eudoxia, 104
Eulalius, 12
Eusebius, 81
——— of Vercelli, 65
Eustochium, 43, 51, 98, 104
Eutychius, 17
Evangelus, 23
Exuperius, 9

Fabiola, 21
Fall, The, 90
Felicitas, 76
Felix, 12
Fremantle, Dean, 47, 48, 107
Fretela, 22

Gaul, 22
Geranopepa, 2
Getae, 22
———, tent-churches of, 69
Gibbon, 51, 52
Glover, Dr. T. R., 52
Gnosticism, 74
Gore, Bishop, 14–15
Gratian, 70
Gratian's Rescript, 62
Grazers, 41
Gregory of Nazianzus, 3, 9
——— of Nyssa, 105
Grützmacher, 36
Gymnosophists, 48

Hadrian, 15
Harnack, 94
Heathenism, 70
Hedibia, 22
Heliodorus, 67, 106
Helvidius, 67
Heresies, 73–97
Heros, 92
Hexapla, 81
Hilary, 71
Himerius, 58

Ignatius, 56, 59, 60
Indefectibility of Grace, 92
Innocent, 13, 62, 91
Irenaeus, 57, 75

Jerome, St., his claim to attention, vii, viii
———, St., his interpretations, 23
———, St., as a teacher, 24, 43
———, St., as a translator, 27, 28, 34–37
John of Jerusalem, 19, 62, 79, 82, 84, 92
Josephus, 25
Judith, Book of, 107
Julian of Antioch, 9
——— the Apostate, 5, 66, 71
——— (nobleman), 103
Justin Martyr, 64

Kidd, Dr. B. J., 16, 25, 41, 59, 88

Laeta, 67
Lazarus of Aix, 92
Lent, 43, 77, 78, 105
Leo I., 58, 59, 70
Lerins, 65
Lightfoot, Bishop, 12, 13, 14
Lucinius, 99, 106

Macarius, 80
——— of Alexandria, 40
Maclear, Dr. G. F., 69, 71
Manuscript, Sinaitic, 29

INDEX

Marcella, 21, 29, 33, 44, 76, 80, 98
Marcellinus. *See* Ammianus
Marcus, 101
Marnas, 68
Maximilla, 75, 78
Milman, Dean, 35, 55, 63
Minervius, 22
Mithraism, 68
Modalists, 77
Monasticism, 38–53
Monophysites, 40
Montanism, 74–79
Moule, Bp., 54
Mysteries, 70

Nectarius, 4
Neoplatonism, 16
Nepotian, 9
Nicaea, Council of, 11, 66
Nicetas of Remesiana, 99
Nitria, 39, 40, 79
Non-communicating attendance, 100

Oceanus, 83
Onasus of Segeste, 108
Orange, Council of, 92
Orders, Holy, 10
Ordinands, 19
Ordinations, forced, 18
Origen, 79–88
Orosius, 92, 97, 108

Pachomius, 39
Palladius, 40
Pammachius, 18, 35, 47, 67, 83, 84
Pantaenus, 48
Papacy, 9, 56–63
Paphnutius, 17
Paul of Samosata, 4
Paula, 20, 21, 47, 51, 66, 81, 98, 105, 106
——, the younger, 33
Paulinian, 19
Paulinus, 43
Pelagianism, 88–97
Pepuza, 75
" Perdition, Mass of," 92

Περί 'Αρχῶν, 87
Perpetua, 76
Petrine claims, 57, 58
Pharisees, 80
Philo, 86
Pilgrimages, 104
Pipizo, 2
Pispir, 39
Poemen, 16
Pontifex Maximus, 70
Praetextatus, 55
Praxeas, 75
Prayer of departed for living, 105
Predestination, 92
Presbyters, 12
—— of Alexandria, 13–18
Principia, 22
Prisca, 75
Proba, 3, 6
Proclus, 77
Psalter, Jerome's Latin, 22
Ptolemy, 25

Quinta, 31

Relics, 103–4
Remoboth, 42
Reservation, 100
Rhetitius, 21
Rhetoric, study of, 71
Rome, Church of, 56–63
——, Jerome's two attitudes to, 62, 63
——, fall of, 63, 108
Rufinus, 82, 84, 87
—— (Syrian), 89
Ruskin, 36
Rusticus, 9

Sabellius, 77
Sabinianus, 7
Saints' Days, 105
Sarabaitae, 42
Sauses, 42
Scete, 39
Scriptures, Canon of, 87
——, study of, 20–24
——, text of, 24–30
Seasons of the Church, 105

INDEX

Semi-Pelagianism, 96
Senate, 71, 81
Septuagint, 31–33
Serapis, 68
Severus of Antioch, 17
Shepherd of Hermas, 8
Simeon Stylites, 41
Sin, original, 90
Siricius, 80
Socrates, 99
Sozomen, 11
Stewart, Rev. H. F., 100, 102
Subintroductae, 7
Sunnias, 22
Symmachus, 31

Tertullian, 64, 76, 78, 83
Texts, state of Greek, Hebrew, and Latin, 24–30
Theodora, 106
Theodore of Mopsuestia, 89
Theodotion, 31
Theophilus, 79, 80, 82, 84, 98, 99
Thierry, 30
Toxotius, 47

"Translators to the Reader," A. V., 36–37
Turner, Mr. C. H., 12, 16, 18, 57

Ulphilas, 64
Ursinus, 12, 56

Valens, 66
Valentinian I., edict of, 3
Veredarius, 2, 5
Versions, Latin, 24–25
Vigilantius, 4, 27, 108
Vincent, 19, 98
Virginity, 44–46
Vitalis, 96
Vulgate, 28, 34, 36, 107, 109

Westcott, Bishop, 35
Women, Roman, 49–50
Wordsworth, Bishop John, 14
Wordsworth and White, 28, 29

Zosimus, 91

INDEX TO LETTERS
OF ST. JEROME QUOTED IN THE FOREGOING PAGES

Letter i, 108
,, vi, 9
,, vii, 9, 47
,, xiv, 41, 42, 106
,, xv, 58
,, xvi, 58
,, xvii, 42, 100, 101
,, xviii, 21, 26
,, xix, 20
,, xx, 33
,, xxi, 21
,, xxii, 1, 2, 5, 7, 8, 42, 43, 44, 45, 47
,, xxiv, 44, 45
,, xxv, 21
,, xxvi, 21
,, xxvii, 26, 29
,, xxviii, 21, 33
,, xxxi, 105
,, xxxiii, 81
,, xxxv, 21
,, xxxvi, 39, 82
,, xxxvii, 21
,, xxxviii, 44
,, xxxix, 22, 49, 106
,, xl, 108
,, xli, 76, 78
,, xlv, 63
,, xlvi, 66, 98, 104
,, xlviii, 98, 100
,, xlix, 35
,, li, 19, 73, 79, 84, 98
,, lii, 2, 4, 6, 11, 20
,, liv, 22
,, lvi, 13, 23, 32
,, lvii, 34

Letter lviii, 12, 105
,, lix, 21
,, lx, 9, 67
,, lxiii, 62
,, lxv, 22
,, lxvi, 67
,, lxvii, 13
,, lxix, 12, 17, 101
,, lxx, 48
,, lxxi, 33, 99
,, lxxiii, 23
,, lxxiv, 23
,, lxxv, 22, 106
,, lxxvii, 21
,, lxxviii, 21
,, lxxx, 82
,, lxxxi, 82
,, lxxxii, 82, 83, 84
,, lxxxiv, 83, 85
,, lxxxv, 83
,, xcii, 79, 84
,, civ, 13, 20, 27, 30, 32
,, cvi, 22, 25, 33
,, cvii, 33, 45, 67, 105
,, cviii, 20, 22, 104, 105
,, cix, 108, 104
,, cxii, 20, 30
,, cxiv, 98
,, cxvii, 7, 8, 49, 52
,, cxviii, 103
,, cxx, 22
,, cxxi, 22
,, cxxiii, 44
,, cxxiv, 84
,, cxxv, 9, 19, 60, 99
,, cxxvi, 63

INDEX TO LETTERS

Letter cxxvii, 21, 47, 49, 62, 63, 80
„ cxxviii, 49, 63, 108
„ cxxx, 3, 45, 46, 101
„ cxxxiii, 78, 92, 94
„ cxxxv, 13

Letter cxxxvii, 62
„ cxxxviii, 92
„ cxxxix, 22
„ cxl, 22
„ cxlvi, 11, 12, 13, 62, 98
„ cxlvii, 7

www.ingramcontent.com/pod-product-compliance
Lightning Source LLC
Chambersburg PA
CBHW070507100426
42743CB00010B/1780